Guide to Millions

Copyright

© Dan Horvat, 2024

All rights reserved. No part of this book may be reproduced, stored in a retrieval system, or transmitted in any form or by any means, electronic, mechanical, photocopying, recording, or otherwise, without the prior written permission of the publisher, except in the case of brief quotations embodied in critical articles and reviews.

Published by Dan Horvat
Level 17, 2 Chifley Tower, Sydney, NSW 2000
ISBN: 978-1-7636802-1-0
First Edition: August 2024
Cover design by Cover Palette
Edited by Dan Horvat
For more information about Dan Horvat, visit www.horvatcapital.com.au.

Disclaimer: The information provided in this book is for educational and informational purposes only. It is not intended as financial, investment, or legal advice. The strategies and recommendations outlined in this book are based on personal experiences and research and may not be suitable for all individuals or situations. Before making any financial or investment decisions, it is strongly advised that you consult with a licensed financial advisor or other qualified professionals. The author and publisher are not responsible for any losses or damages that may occur as a result of following the suggestions or strategies discussed in this book. Investing involves risk, including the potential loss of principal, and there is no guarantee of future performance.

CONTENTS

INTRODUCTION
Preface...7
Why This Guide?..8
Understanding the Strategy..10
The Roadmap..11
Who Can Benefit from This Guide?..13
The Story of Dan Horvat...15

PART 1. OVERVIEW OF THE WORLD
Monetary System and Businesses..20
Strategic Investments..31
Who can you be in this world?..35
The Smart Approach: Saving and Investing.....................................41
Beyond Being a Worker..45
Becoming a Business Owner..49
Embracing Passive Ownership...53
The Allure of the Stock Market...58
The Goal: Passive Income and Financial Independence...................62
The Ultimate Guide to Financial Freedom.......................................65

PART 2. – WEALTH BUILDING TOOLS
BASICS OF SAVING..70
    The Role of Income
    Choosing an Occupation:
    Income Levels
    Minimizing Expenses
    The Power of Early Savings

THE FUNDAMENTALS OF INVESTING 79
    The Fundamentals of Investing
    Understanding Investing
    Types of Investments
    Property Investments
    Business Investments
    Expected Returns on Different Investment Vehicles
    Comparing Returns Over Time
    Becoming a Millionaire Through Investing

BANKS 90
    Introduction to Banking
    The Basics of Banking
    How Banks Grant Loans
    Why Banks Prefer Lending for Real Estate
    Types of Real Estate Loans
    The Role of Banks in the Real Estate Market
    How Banks Finance Businesses
    The Role of Banks in Business Operations
    Types of Business Loans
    The Role of Banks in Financing Business Operations

LEVERAGE 107
    Introduction to Leverage
    How Leverage Works in General
    Leverage in Property Investment
    Calculating Returns with Leverage
    Impact of Leverage on Returns
    Advantages of Using Leverage in Property Investment
    Risks of Using Leverage in Property Investment
    Mitigating Risks of Leverage

Example

PROPERTY INVESTING..113
    Property Investing Basics: Leveraging for Higher Returns
    Maximizing Returns by Paying More Than the Minimum Loan Amount
    Avoiding the Dream Home Trap
    Understanding Capital Appreciation in Property Investment
    The Impact of Minimum Deposit on Property Investment Returns
    Implications for Further Property Investments
    The Power of Equity Building in Multiple Property Investments

BUSINESS INVESTING..135
    The Vital Role of Businesses in the Economy
    Types of Businesses
    Economic Sectors and Industries
    Investing in Listed Equities: A Comprehensive Guide
    Investing in Private Businesses
    Investing in Small Private Businesses
    Passive Investment Strategy
    Comparing Private Business Investments with Listed Equities

FINANCIAL LITERACY..161
    Essential Knowledge for Investing in Property and Businesses
    Integrating Knowledge for Investment Success

PART 3. - DETAILED ROADMAP
ACHIEVING MILLIONAIRE STATUS..166

INCREASING YOUR INCOME...171
    Trade Occupations: Start Earning Early
    Professional Careers: Delayed Gratification

Guide to Millions

    Making Your Earnings Count
    Overcoming Barriers to Success
    Reality Check

MNIMINIZE YOUR EXPENSES..175
    Accommodation
    Food
    Transport
    Entertainment
    Travel

INVEST IN PROPERTY..192
    You Don't Need to Live Where You Buy
    Discovering The Ideal Investment Property
    Short-Term Accommodation and Tourism
    What COVID-19 Taught Me About Investing in Property

INVEST IN PRIVATE EQUITY..211
    Identifying Good Small Businesses for Private Equity Investment
    Understanding Multiples in Private Business Valuation
    Assessing Profitability in Small Businesses for Investment
    Key Industries for Small Businesses
    Investing in Small Businesses – Lessons from COVID-19
    Identifying Good Entry Points for Small Private Business Investments

THE POWER OF LEVERAGE AND THE ART OF BUYOUT.......................240

PART 3. GROUP INVESTING

THE POWER OF GROUP INVESTING..243
    The Concept of Group Investing
    Benefits of Group Investing

Setting Up a Group Investment
   Finding and Evaluating Investment Opportunities
   The Importance of Shared Ideas

FAMILY-DRIVEN INVESTING..250
   The Power of a Family Portfolio
   A Different Approach: Individual Jobs and Shared Investments
   Steps to Implement Family-Driven Investing
   Examples of Successful Family-Driven Investing
   Overcoming Potential Challenges

FAMILY OFFICES AND LEGACY BUILDING..256
   Understanding Family Offices
   Protecting Wealth through Family Trusts
   Professional Management in Family Offices
   Building a Legacy with Family Offices

HELP WITH INVESTING...261

INTRODUCTION

Preface

Welcome to the journey of becoming a millionaire, a path that is accessible to anyone, regardless of your background, education, or specialized skills. This book is designed to be a practical, straightforward guide that demystifies the process of wealth creation. It is not about abstract concepts or untested theories, but about real, actionable steps that you can follow to achieve financial success.

In the pages that follow, you will find a wealth of knowledge distilled into clear and concise steps. This guide is meant to be your companion on the road to financial independence, providing you with the tools and insights you need to navigate the complex world of personal finance and investments. Whether you are starting from scratch or looking to enhance your existing financial strategies, this book is tailored to meet you where you are and guide you towards where you want to be.

The journey to becoming a millionaire is not a sprint but a marathon. It requires patience, discipline, and a commitment to making informed decisions. This guide breaks down the process into manageable steps, ensuring that you can progress steadily without feeling overwhelmed. Each chapter is designed to build on the previous one, creating a comprehensive roadmap that you can follow at your own pace.

As you embark on this journey, remember that wealth creation is not reserved for the few. It is within your reach, and with the right guidance and determination, you can achieve financial freedom. This book aims to empower you with the knowledge and confidence to take control of your financial future. Welcome to your path to becoming a millionaire. Let's embark on this transformative journey together, turning your financial dreams into reality.

Why This Guide?

Many books promise the secret to becoming rich, often wrapped in vague notions of resilience, mindset, and other intangible qualities. While these attributes can be beneficial, they often leave readers with more questions than answers. This guide, however, is different. It provides a clear roadmap, answering the "why" behind each step, and then detailing the "how" in a simple, easy-to-follow manner. Think of it as a manual similar to those that guide you through obtaining a university degree—concrete steps that, when followed, lead to a specific outcome. Since we are born, we have a very structured life: we go to childcare, then to primary school, then to secondary school, then to high school, then to university. And then the structured journey ends. At this point, we are expected to get employed, and that's it. One common path people consider is progressing in their career to higher levels of management, hoping for a better pay check. However, with a better pay check often come higher spending habits, a more expensive lifestyle, and additional financial obligations, such as a growing family. Many people find themselves feeling lost, living from day to day, week to week, without any plan or purpose, and without any structured plan to achieve their financial goals. Most people want to be rich, not just to afford nicer things, but also to achieve financial independence so they no longer need to work. Yet, the path to this goal often remains unclear. Many are scared to even try anything new because they don't know much about it or are simply afraid of the risks involved. Those few who are willing to take the plunge often feel like they're jumping into the unknown, unsure of what they're getting into.

That's why I'm writing this guide. It is not just my opinion based on my 'feelings,' but a summation of my experiences and an overview of the world we live in. It offers a straightforward plan of action for anyone. We live in a monetary world, and we need to make it work for us. This guide provides the structured plan you need after the traditional path of education ends. Instead of leaving you to figure it out on your own, it lays out each step in a logical sequence, much like the education system did in your early years. The goal is to demystify the process of

Guide to Millions

becoming a millionaire in 10 years by breaking it down into manageable steps that anyone can follow. This structured approach ensures that you understand not only what to do but why you're doing it, making each action purposeful and clear. By following this guide, you'll be able to navigate the complexities of financial growth with confidence, avoiding the common pitfalls that often derail many well-meaning but poorly informed attempts at wealth building. You'll learn how to increase your income, minimize expenses, and invest wisely in property and businesses. You'll gain the knowledge and skills necessary to take calculated risks, rather than blind leaps of faith. In essence, this guide is about providing you with the tools and knowledge to build a secure financial future systematically. It's about creating a clear, structured path to financial independence, allowing you to live life on your terms. So, take a deep breath, follow the steps laid out in this book, and embark on your journey to becoming a millionaire in 10 years or less. You have the roadmap; now it's time to take the first step.

Understanding the Strategy

Before diving into the step-by-step guide, it's important to understand the foundation of the strategy. This guide is based on the principle that wealth creation is a systematic process that anyone can master. Simply put, it involves saving and investing. It's about making informed choices and taking deliberate actions. We will explore how the world operates as a monetary system, understanding how to participate effectively and make it work to our advantage. Additionally, we will examine the roles we can assume in this world, specifically the two primary economic roles: the worker and the owner. Understanding these roles is crucial because your path to becoming a millionaire involves transitioning from being solely a worker to also becoming an owner and investor. We will discuss what investing entails, the various types of investments available, and how each of the main investment vehicles functions. Once you grasp the background that informs our rational decisions, we will proceed to a practical guide on how to implement these strategies effectively.

Guide to Millions

The Roadmap

1. Understanding How the World Works:

We start by exploring the basics of what the world consists of and how it functions, focusing on economic principles and how money flows in society. This will give you a solid understanding of the larger system you are operating within. By comprehending how the world operates and identifying the roles we can assume, you will have a broader view and a clearer picture of the possibilities ahead. You will be looking at the whole board game instead of just the next space in front of you. We will examine what investing is and how it works, so you understand what constitutes good growth and returns. We will cover the main investment vehicles—property and businesses—and analyse the intricacies of each and how they compare. Once we understand the world and recognize how we can become wealthy through investing, we need to work out how to start investing and how to gather the money to begin.

2. Saving Money:

The first actionable step is learning how to save effectively. This section covers two main aspects—increasing your income and budgeting by cutting unnecessary expenses and developing a savings mindset. Saving money is the foundation upon which your investment strategy will be built. Additionally, we will discuss how to avoid lifestyle inflation. By mastering the art of saving, you will create a financial cushion that allows you to invest confidently and weather economic downturns.

3. Investing Wisely:

Here, we delve into the world of investments. You will learn about different types of investments, such as stocks, real estate, and businesses, and how to evaluate their potential. We will explore how each of these investments works and the benefits of each. This section will help you identify good investment opportunities and avoid common pitfalls. We will cover the basics of stock market investing, including the importance of diversification, understanding risk tolerance, and the power of compound interest. In real estate, we will discuss strategies for finding undervalued properties, understanding cash flow, and leveraging financing to maximize returns. For business investments, we will explore how to assess a business's financial health, market position, and growth potential. By gaining a comprehensive understanding of these investment avenues, you will be able to build a diversified portfolio that aligns with your financial goals.

4. Step-by-Step Guide

Finally, this guide culminates in a detailed plan for starting your investment journey with limited funds. You'll learn how to leverage small amounts of money into significant investments, gradually building your wealth over time. Additionally, we will discuss the importance of reinvesting returns and seeking out low-cost investment options. By following this step-by-step approach, you will see that even modest investments can grow substantially with time and disciplined effort.

Understanding these principles and steps will equip you with the knowledge and confidence to navigate the financial landscape. This guide aims to demystify the process of wealth creation, providing you with a clear and actionable roadmap. By transitioning from a worker to an owner/investor, you can harness the power of the economic system to build substantial wealth and achieve financial independence.

Who Can Benefit from This Guide?

This book is for everyone—whether you are just starting your career, looking to make a change, or simply wanting to improve your financial situation. The steps outlined here require no prior knowledge or specialized skills. They are designed to be easy to understand and implement, ensuring that anyone can follow them and achieve success.

Whether you are a recent graduate entering the workforce for the first time, a mid-career professional seeking to enhance your financial stability, or someone nearing retirement who wants to maximize your wealth, this guide offers valuable insights and actionable steps tailored to your needs. It's crafted to demystify the complexities of personal finance and investment, breaking down concepts into simple, manageable steps that anyone can grasp.

For young professionals just starting out, this book provides a roadmap to establish a solid financial foundation early on, allowing you to avoid common pitfalls and build wealth from the ground up. It teaches the importance of saving and investing wisely from the beginning, setting the stage for long-term financial success.

For those considering a career change, this guide offers strategies to navigate the transition smoothly while keeping your financial goals on track. It covers ways to manage your finances during periods of change and uncertainty, ensuring that you stay focused on your path to wealth creation.

For individuals looking to improve their current financial situation, this book presents practical methods to optimize your income, reduce unnecessary expenses, and invest wisely. It encourages a mindset shift towards financial discipline and strategic planning, empowering you to take control of your financial future.

Even if you have limited financial literacy or are sceptical about your ability to manage money effectively, this guide is designed with you in mind. The language is straightforward, avoiding jargon and technical terms, making it accessible to everyone regardless of their background or experience.

Ultimately, this guide is for anyone who desires financial independence and is willing to take proactive steps to achieve it. By following the clear, actionable steps outlined in this book, you can transform your financial situation and work towards becoming a millionaire in ten years or less.

Becoming a millionaire is not reserved for the elite or those with insider knowledge. It is a goal that is within reach for anyone willing to follow a clear, structured plan. This guide provides you with that plan. By understanding the principles, making smart choices, and taking consistent action, you can achieve financial freedom and transform your life.

This journey is about more than just accumulating wealth—it's about empowering yourself to make informed financial decisions that can lead to lasting security and independence. The strategies outlined in this guide are practical and proven, designed to be accessible to individuals from all walks of life. Whether you're a recent graduate, a working professional, or someone looking to enhance your financial knowledge, this book offers a step-by-step approach to building and growing your wealth.

The key to success lies in your willingness to learn and apply the principles consistently. Each chapter provides detailed insights and actionable steps, from understanding the economic system to mastering the art of saving and investing. With dedication and perseverance, you will see tangible results as your financial situation improves.

If you are ready to take control of your financial future, let's begin this journey together. Follow the steps, stay committed, and watch as your wealth grows. Embrace the process, and don't be discouraged by setbacks. Instead, view them as opportunities to learn and refine your approach. Welcome to your path to becoming a millionaire. Your financial freedom is within reach, and this guide is here to help you every step of the way.

Guide to Millions

The Story of Dan Horvat: From Croatia to Financial Independence

Hello, my name is Dan Horvat. My journey from a small town in Croatia to becoming financially independent in Australia is a story of determination, learning, and strategic investing. I want to share my story to inspire and guide others on their path to financial success.

Early Life in Croatia

I was born and raised in Croatia, in the former Yugoslavia, where the socialist environment shaped my early years. This setting had a profound impact on how people, including my parents, viewed money and investments. The prevalent mindset was to live day by day, without any thought of wealth creation or financial planning. The idea of investing was virtually non-existent. Those with better incomes would simply save money under their mattresses, without any plans to grow it.

Growing up, I often faced the question, "What do you want to be when you grow up?" Unlike my peers who had clear-cut answers like becoming a policeman, doctor, or construction worker, I always said, "I just want to play." This innocent desire was more than just a child's wish; it reflected my deeper yearning for a life free from financial constraints.

Aspirations and Early Influences

During my childhood, I spent a lot of time with my grandfather, who was a veterinarian. I accompanied him to neighbouring villages, where he tended to various animals. His work fascinated me, and for a while, I aspired to follow in his footsteps. However, as I grew older, around the age of 15, I began to understand the broader world and realized that to truly "just play" and enjoy life, I needed financial independence. I concluded that becoming a millionaire was the way to achieve this.

The question then was, how do I become a millionaire? I had no clear answer, but I knew I needed to work in an environment related to investments or the stock market. The idea of Wall Street, inspired by movies, intrigued me. This led me to pursue higher education in Economics.

Higher Education in the USA

I was fortunate that my parents could afford to send me to Webster University in the USA, where I studied Economics. This experience was eye-opening and transformative. While the education I received was excellent, I realized that I could have gained similar knowledge at a Croatian university. The true value of studying in the USA was the exposure to a capitalist mindset and the understanding of how investments and the financial market operate.

Early Career in Croatia

After completing my studies, I returned to Croatia and began my career as a financial auditor with Deloitte. This role was immensely insightful, providing me with a deep understanding of the intricacies of financial systems and business operations. I was responsible for examining and verifying companies' financial records, which gave me a solid foundation in auditing principles and practices. Concurrently, I enrolled in the MBA program at the Zagreb University Faculty of Economics. This decision was driven by my desire to broaden my business acumen and gain a more comprehensive understanding of economic theories and management strategies.

While working as an auditor, I developed a keen interest in investments and asset management, which led me to transition into a managerial position at a real estate investment fund. This new role allowed me to further expand my knowledge in investment strategies, property valuation, and portfolio management. I gained valuable experience in assessing market trends, identifying lucrative investment opportunities, and managing assets to maximize returns.

Despite these promising roles and the valuable experience I was gaining, I soon realized that the economic conditions and salary scales in Croatia made it nearly impossible to save enough money to invest and grow wealth. The country was still grappling with the aftermath of the Global Economic Crisis (GEC) of the early 2010s, which had a significant impact on its economy. The GEC led to high unemployment rates, stagnant wages, and limited job opportunities, particularly in the financial sector. These conditions severely restricted my ability to accumulate the necessary capital for meaningful investments.

Recognizing the limitations of my financial growth in Croatia, I made the difficult decision to seek opportunities abroad. I needed to find a place with a higher standard of living and better prospects for savings and investments. This move was crucial in my journey towards financial independence and wealth creation. The experience and knowledge I gained in Croatia laid a strong foundation for my future endeavours, but it was clear that I needed to explore new horizons to achieve my financial goals.

Immigration to Australia

Driven by the need for a higher living standard, I decided to immigrate to Australia. I arrived with just a few thousand dollars in my pocket, but I was determined to make the most of the opportunities that lay ahead. Australia's dynamic economy and high-paying jobs provided the perfect environment for me to build my savings and start investing.

Initially, finding a good role in asset management proved challenging. I had to pivot and started working in construction. Through hard work and perseverance, I worked my way up to a high-paying position. This experience taught me the value of adaptability and resilience in the face of challenges.

Overcoming Personal Challenges

My journey was not without personal challenges. Before moving to Australia, I went through a difficult divorce. This period of emotional turmoil taught me the importance of resilience and maintaining a positive outlook, even during tough times.

From my first marriage, I have two beautiful children, Tristan and Korinna. They have been a significant part of my journey and one of the reasons I decided to write this book. I want to help them understand the world better and guide them in choosing their direction in life.

After settling in Australia, I faced another significant challenge: a battle with testicular cancer. Thanks to modern medicine and early detection, I was able to overcome this health crisis. This experience underscored the importance of health and the need to stay strong, both physically and mentally, to achieve long-term goals.

To add to these challenges, I also survived a motorcycle accident. Each of these incidents, while difficult, reinforced my determination to succeed and reminded me of the importance of perseverance.

A New Chapter: Family and Support

In Australia, I remarried and had another beautiful daughter, Kiara. My wife, Stela, has been a pillar of support throughout all our personal and business challenges. Her unwavering support and belief in me have been crucial in overcoming the hurdles we faced. I am incredibly thankful to have her by my side throughout this journey. Her presence and encouragement have been instrumental in our shared success.

The Path to Financial Independence

My journey to becoming financially independent within ten years of arriving in Australia was marked by strategic planning and smart investing. I started by saving diligently from my high-paying job and made informed investment decisions. My investments were primarily in property and businesses. Each investment was carefully researched and aligned with my financial goals.

One of the key lessons I learned was the power of compounding and the importance of starting early. Even with modest savings, the right investments can grow significantly over time. I also learned the value of leveraging opportunities and making the most of the resources available.

Changing Mindsets

One of the most significant challenges I faced was changing my mindset from the one I grew up with to a capitalist approach. This shift was crucial for my financial success. Understanding the importance of investments and wealth creation was a game-changer. It not only transformed my life but also inspired me to help others, especially young people, to see the possibilities that smart investing can offer.

Conclusion: Sharing My Knowledge

Today, I am proud of the financial independence I have achieved. My journey from Croatia to becoming financially independent in Australia is a testament to the power of strategic investing and the right mindset. My goal now is to share the knowledge and strategies that helped me succeed.

I believe that anyone can achieve financial success with the right guidance and a clear plan. My book aims to provide a simple, step-by-step guide to becoming a millionaire. It's not about having specialized skills, secret sauces, or extraordinary talents. It's about making informed decisions, starting early, and staying committed to your financial goals.

If you're starting your occupational and life journey, I want to help you understand the world better and show you how easy it can be to become wealthy. Let's embark on this journey together and transform your financial future.

PART 1.
OVERVIEW – HOW THE WORLD WORKS

Chapter 1.1
Understanding the Monetary System and How Everything Works Through Businesses

Understanding the Financial World

In order to make informed decisions about our financial future, we first need to understand the world we live in. More specifically, we need to grasp the intricacies of the monetary system and the pivotal role businesses play within it. Our existence and interactions in the modern world are fundamentally intertwined with this system, and recognizing this is the first step towards financial literacy and success.

The monetary system forms the backbone of our economy, influencing how money is created, distributed, and utilized. It governs the flow of capital, affecting everything from individual savings accounts to multinational investments. To navigate this system effectively, one must understand key concepts such as inflation, interest rates, and currency valuation. These elements dictate the purchasing power of our money and the value of our investments over time. Without a solid grasp of these principles, making sound financial decisions becomes a daunting task.

Businesses, on the other hand, are the engines driving economic growth. They create jobs, generate income, and spur innovation. Understanding how businesses operate—how they generate revenue, manage expenses, and invest in growth—is crucial for anyone looking to build wealth. This knowledge allows us to make informed choices about where to invest our money. It helps us discern which companies are likely to thrive and which might falter, guiding our investment strategies towards those that offer the best potential returns.

Moreover, recognizing the interdependence between the monetary system and businesses is essential. Businesses rely on the monetary system for capital, whether through loans, investments, or market operations. In turn, the health of the monetary system is often reflected in the performance of businesses. Economic policies, regulatory frameworks, and market dynamics all interplay to shape the financial landscape. By understanding these relationships, we can better anticipate market trends and position ourselves to take advantage of emerging opportunities.

Financial literacy extends beyond personal finance. It encompasses a comprehensive understanding of the economic environment in which we live. This includes being aware of global economic trends, geopolitical factors, and technological advancements that can impact markets. Staying informed about these broader issues empowers us to make proactive and strategic financial decisions.

Recognizing the importance of the monetary system and the role of businesses within it is foundational to achieving financial success. By deepening our understanding of these elements, we equip ourselves with the knowledge needed to navigate the complexities of the financial world. This informed perspective enables us to make smarter choices, maximize our investment potential, and ultimately, secure a prosperous financial future.

Living in a Monetary World

We live in a monetary world. Unlike self-sufficient farmers of the past who could rely solely on their land, modern life depends heavily on financial resources. Even today's farmers participate in the economy by selling their produce and using the money earned to purchase necessities. Money serves as the essential medium of exchange that enables trade, making it vital to grasp its importance. If someone chooses not to adapt to the monetary system, they might have to retreat to a completely self-sustained life in the wilderness.

In the past, bartering was the primary method of trade. People exchanged goods and services directly, which worked well in small, self-contained communities. However, as societies grew and economies became more complex, the limitations of bartering became apparent. It was inefficient and cumbersome, requiring a double coincidence of wants—finding someone who had what you needed and who also needed what you had. The invention of money revolutionized trade by introducing a common medium of exchange, allowing for more efficient and widespread economic activity.

Today, money is central to almost every aspect of our lives. We earn money through work or investments and use it to buy goods and services, pay taxes, save for the future, and invest. It acts as a store of value, a unit of account, and a standard of deferred payment. These functions make it indispensable in our daily lives and in the broader economy. Understanding how money works—how it is created, managed, and its value determined—is essential for making informed financial decisions.

The modern financial system is complex, encompassing banks, markets, and regulatory institutions. Banks, for instance, play a critical role by providing a safe place for savings and offering loans to individuals and businesses. They facilitate transactions and help in the creation of money through lending. Financial markets allow for the buying and selling of assets like stocks, bonds, and real estate, enabling wealth accumulation and distribution. Regulatory bodies ensure the stability and integrity of the financial system, protecting consumers and maintaining trust in the monetary system.

Moreover, the global nature of today's economy means that money flows across borders with ease. International trade and investment are fundamental to economic growth and development, but they also introduce complexities like currency exchange rates and international financial regulations. Understanding these global financial dynamics is crucial for anyone looking to navigate the modern economy successfully.

Living in a monetary world also means that financial literacy is more important than ever. It involves not just understanding how to manage personal finances but also grasping broader economic principles. By recognizing the role of money in our lives and the economy, we can better appreciate its value and make more strategic decisions about earning, spending, saving, and investing. This knowledge empowers us to take control of our financial future, ensuring that we can navigate the complexities of the monetary world with confidence and competence.

Money is the cornerstone of modern life, influencing everything from individual daily transactions to the functioning of the global economy. Understanding its role and the systems that support **it is essential for anyone aiming to achieve financial stability and success.**

The Mechanism of Trade

The foundation of our monetary system is trade. Everything in our economy functions through the exchange of goods and services for money. This fundamental concept of trade underpins all economic activities, shaping the way we interact and conduct transactions. Trade facilitates the movement of goods and services from producers to consumers, and it is through this exchange that value is created and distributed within the economy.

In the modern economy, trade occurs primarily through businesses. These entities act as intermediaries between individuals who produce goods or offer services and those who consume them. Businesses provide a structured and efficient platform for transactions, handling everything from marketing and sales to logistics and customer service. For example, while an individual might offer lawn mowing services, they often do so through a small business, which handles scheduling, billing, and other administrative tasks. This organization not only streamlines the process but also allows for scalability and consistency in service delivery.

Even seemingly straightforward services like window cleaning are typically managed through business operations. Small business enterprises often organize these services to ensure they meet quality standards, comply with regulations, and offer competitive pricing. This structure enables service providers to reach a broader customer base and manage operational complexities more effectively than if they were working independently.

The role of businesses extends beyond just facilitating trade; they also drive economic growth and innovation. They create jobs, generate income, and contribute to the overall economic development of a region. By organizing and optimizing trade processes, businesses enhance efficiency, reduce transaction costs, and foster a competitive market environment.

Furthermore, businesses play a crucial role in the supply chain, sourcing materials, managing inventory, and distributing products. They are integral to the functioning of various industries, from manufacturing and retail to services and technology. By efficiently coordinating these elements, businesses ensure that goods and services are available to meet consumer demand and that the flow of trade remains uninterrupted.

The mechanism of trade is central to our monetary system and the functioning of the economy. Businesses act as vital intermediaries, facilitating the exchange of goods and services and driving economic activity. Understanding this mechanism highlights the importance of businesses in creating value, managing transactions, and supporting economic growth.

Businesses as the Engine of the Economy

Businesses are the engines that drive the economy. They are fundamental to the functioning of economic systems, providing the essential goods and services that meet the diverse needs and wants of consumers. From the groceries we buy to the technology we use, businesses are at the heart of delivering products and services that enhance our daily lives. But who exactly is responsible for producing and delivering these goods and services? The answer lies in the workforce—the people employed by these businesses.

The relationship between businesses and their employees is symbiotic. Businesses rely on a skilled and motivated workforce to operate effectively and efficiently. Employees bring their expertise, labour, and creativity to their roles, contributing to the production, management, and delivery of goods and services. Without this human capital, businesses would struggle to function, innovate, or expand. The workforce encompasses a wide range of roles, from front-line staff and technical experts to managerial and executive positions, each playing a critical part in the business's success.

Most people rely on businesses for employment, making them a primary source of livelihood for the majority of the population. Employment within businesses provides individuals with income, job security, and opportunities for career advancement. It is through these jobs that people can earn money to support themselves and their families, contribute to their communities, and participate in the economy.

Furthermore, businesses not only offer employment but also drive economic growth by creating new opportunities and stimulating investment. They invest in research and development, adopt new technologies, and explore emerging markets, all of which contribute to economic dynamism and progress. By fostering innovation and competition, businesses enhance productivity and efficiency, leading to overall improvements in living standards and quality of life.

In addition to their role in employment and economic growth, businesses are crucial in shaping economic policy and influencing market trends. Their operations impact local economies and global markets, affecting everything from consumer prices to international trade dynamics. Understanding the role of businesses as the engine of the economy underscores their importance in driving economic activity, supporting livelihoods, and shaping the future of economic development.

The Workforce and Income Generation

The workforce is integral to the operation of businesses. Employees are the backbone of any organization, contributing their labour, skills, and expertise to produce goods and provide services. This collaborative effort is essential for the functioning and success of businesses across all industries. In return for their work, employees receive wages, which constitute their income. This income serves as a crucial component of their financial stability, enabling them to support themselves and their families, and to participate actively in the economy.

The flow of income from businesses to employees initiates a vital economic cycle. Employees use their wages to cover personal expenses such as housing, food, transportation, and entertainment. This spending generates demand for various goods and services, thereby creating a continuous cycle of money flow within the economy. This cycle is fundamental to sustaining economic activity and promoting growth. By purchasing products and services, employees not only fulfill their needs but also support other businesses, which in turn may employ additional workers and generate further economic activity.

One of the biggest expenses for any business is the cost of labour. On average, labour costs can account for roughly 50% of a business's total expenses. This significant proportion highlights the critical role of employees within the business ecosystem. The expense of labour includes not only direct wages but also additional costs such as benefits, training, and employee-related taxes. These costs can vary depending on the industry, the nature of the work, and the country in which the business operates. For instance, sectors like manufacturing and technology may have higher labour costs due to specialized skills and advanced training requirements, while service-oriented industries might experience different cost structures.

Understanding the relationship between the workforce and income generation underscores the importance of employees in driving economic performance. Their contributions enable businesses to function and grow, while their spending supports other economic activities. This dynamic interplay between labour costs and consumer spending is essential for maintaining a healthy and resilient economy. As businesses navigate the challenges of labour management and cost control, they must also recognize the value that their workforce brings to their operations and the broader economic landscape.

The Symbiotic Relationship

The relationship between businesses and workers is inherently symbiotic, forming the cornerstone of our economic system. This mutual dependence illustrates how interconnected our economic activities are and how vital each party is to the other. Businesses rely on workers to perform essential functions that allow them to operate and grow. Workers bring their skills, knowledge, and labour to the table, contributing to the production of goods and services that businesses offer. Without this human capital, businesses would struggle to produce or deliver their offerings, ultimately affecting their viability and success.

Conversely, workers depend on businesses for their livelihood. Employment provides individuals with the income necessary to support themselves and their families, fulfill personal needs, and engage in economic activities. This income is crucial for maintaining a standard of living and participating in the broader economy. If businesses were to disappear, workers would lose their primary source of income, leading to a breakdown in their ability to purchase goods and services, which would ripple through the economy and impact various sectors.

This interdependence highlights the integral role each plays in the economic ecosystem. Businesses need a competent and reliable workforce to function efficiently, while workers need stable employment and fair compensation to thrive. Together, this symbiotic relationship drives economic growth, supports consumer spending, and sustains the cycle of economic activity. Understanding this mutual reliance underscores the importance of nurturing both business operations and workforce well-being to foster a robust and resilient economy.

The Flow of Money

The flow of money in the economy is a dynamic and continuous process that starts with businesses. These entities generate revenue by offering goods and services to consumers. This revenue is crucial for their survival and growth, allowing businesses to cover their operational costs, invest in new projects, and expand their activities. Among these costs, one of the most significant is employee wages. Businesses pay their employees for their labour, skills, and expertise, which is essential for maintaining productivity and delivering quality products and services.

Once employees receive their wages, they enter the next phase of the economic cycle. They use this income to purchase goods and services for their personal use, such as groceries, housing, transportation, and entertainment. This spending is vital as it creates demand for the goods and services provided by businesses. When employees spend their earnings, they contribute to the revenue streams of other businesses, thereby stimulating further economic activity.

This cycle of earning and spending is what sustains the economy and drives its growth. As businesses receive revenue from sales, they can reinvest in their operations, hire more employees, and develop new products or services. This reinvestment often leads to increased employment opportunities and higher wages, which in turn boosts consumer spending and demand.

Moreover, this continuous flow of money is crucial for maintaining economic stability. When businesses thrive and employees are compensated well, the economy experiences growth and prosperity.

Conversely, disruptions in this cycle, such as economic downturns or layoffs, can lead to reduced spending, lower demand, and slower economic growth. Therefore, understanding this flow of money helps to appreciate how interconnected our economic activities are and highlights the importance of maintaining a healthy balance between business revenue and consumer spending to ensure sustained economic vitality.

Understanding Your Role

To navigate the monetary system effectively and achieve financial success, it's crucial to understand your role within this system. Every individual operates within the economic framework as either a worker or a business owner. Each role plays a significant part in the economic ecosystem, but they offer distinct pathways for financial growth and wealth accumulation.

As a worker, you contribute your labour and skills to businesses in exchange for wages. This income is your primary source of financial support, enabling you to meet your daily needs and cover personal expenses. However, while earning wages is fundamental, relying solely on this income might not lead to substantial financial growth or wealth creation. To enhance your financial prospects, it's essential to look beyond just earning a salary and explore additional avenues for growing your wealth.

Investing offers one of the most effective ways to build wealth. By putting your money into various investment vehicles, you can leverage the potential of the monetary system to generate additional income and capital appreciation. Investing can take many forms, including purchasing stocks, which allows you to own a share in a company's success; acquiring real estate, which can provide rental income and property value appreciation; or starting your own business, which offers the potential for significant financial returns through entrepreneurial ventures.

Each investment option has its own risks and rewards, and understanding these can help you make informed decisions that align with your financial goals. By diversifying your investments and carefully managing your portfolio, you can create multiple streams of income and capitalize on various opportunities for wealth accumulation.

Ultimately, while being a worker provides the initial financial foundation, transitioning into an investor or business owner allows you to tap into the broader wealth creation potential of the monetary system. Recognizing and embracing these roles will empower you to take control of your financial future and work towards achieving your long-term financial goals.

Adapting to the Monetary System

Adapting to the monetary system means understanding how money works and how businesses operate. It means recognizing that businesses are the primary creators of wealth and that your financial success is linked to your ability to engage with this system effectively.

Chapter 1.2
Strategic Investments

Investing wisely is essential for building substantial wealth over time. This process begins with a comprehensive understanding of the investment landscape, including various industries and businesses that exhibit potential for growth. Strategic investments are not just about placing money into any opportunity but about making informed choices based on thorough research and analysis.

To invest wisely, one must first gain insights into market trends and economic indicators. This involves analysing sectors poised for expansion, such as technology, healthcare, or renewable energy. Identifying businesses within these industries that demonstrate strong growth potential and robust financial health is critical. This research can be carried out through reviewing financial statements, assessing management effectiveness, and understanding market dynamics.

Additionally, it's important to recognize and evaluate the risks associated with different investments. Each investment type—whether stocks, bonds, real estate, or startups—carries its own set of risks. For instance, stocks can be volatile and subject to market fluctuations, while real estate investments might face challenges like property management issues or market downturns. By understanding these risks and incorporating them into your decision-making process, you can better manage potential downsides.

Informed decision-making also involves setting clear investment goals and aligning your strategy with these objectives. Whether you are seeking long-term capital appreciation, steady income, or a mix of both, tailoring your investments to your financial goals and risk tolerance is crucial. Regularly reviewing and adjusting your investment portfolio in response to changing market conditions and personal circumstances will help ensure that your strategy remains effective and aligned with your wealth-building objectives.

The Importance of Early Investment

Starting your investment journey early can profoundly impact your financial future, largely due to the power of compound interest. Compound interest refers to the process where the earnings on an investment—whether interest or returns—are reinvested to generate additional earnings over time. This effect causes your investment to grow at an accelerating rate, which can significantly enhance your financial position in the long run.

When you begin investing early, even modest amounts of money can grow substantially due to the compounding effect. For example, investing $100 a month at an average annual return rate of 7% can result in over $1,200,000 after 40 years. The earlier you start, the more time your money has to grow, and the less you need to invest each month to reach your financial goals.

Early investment also allows you to take advantage of market fluctuations over time. By investing consistently, you benefit from dollar-cost averaging, which means you purchase more shares when prices are low and fewer when prices are high, reducing the impact of volatility and smoothing out the cost of your investments.

Moreover, starting early provides you with more time to recover from potential losses and adjust your investment strategy as needed. The longer investment horizon allows you to weather market downturns and capitalize on long-term growth trends. This extended timeframe also gives you the opportunity to learn about investing, refine your strategy, and develop a disciplined approach to wealth accumulation.

Practical Steps to Take

This book is designed to offer a clear, step-by-step guide on navigating the monetary system and making strategic investments, akin to following a structured path to earn a university degree. The journey to becoming a millionaire involves understanding fundamental financial principles, identifying lucrative investment opportunities, and making informed decisions based on careful analysis.

The first step in this structured path is gaining a solid grasp of money management and business fundamentals. This includes learning about budgeting, saving, and understanding how money flows within the economy. Familiarizing yourself with basic investment concepts, such as asset allocation, risk management, and the types of investment vehicles available, is crucial.

Once you have a foundational understanding, the next step involves identifying and evaluating investment opportunities. Research various sectors and businesses to find those with strong growth potential. Utilize financial tools and resources to analyse investment options and seek out opportunities that align with your financial goals and risk tolerance.

Making informed investment decisions requires ongoing education and vigilance. Stay updated on market trends, economic news, and changes in investment regulations.
Regularly review and adjust your investment strategy to reflect your evolving goals and market conditions.

By following a structured approach, akin to pursuing a degree, you can systematically build your knowledge, develop effective investment strategies, and work towards achieving your financial objectives. This methodical path will guide you through the complexities of the monetary system and set you on a course to financial success and wealth accumulation.

In summary, understanding the monetary system and the role of businesses is crucial for making informed financial decisions. We live in a world where money facilitates trade and businesses are the primary drivers of economic activity. By recognizing your role within this system and learning how to invest wisely, you can achieve financial success. This book will guide you through the process, providing the knowledge and tools you need to become a millionaire. Whether you're just starting your journey or looking to enhance your financial literacy, the insights and strategies shared here will help you reach your goals. So, let's dive in and start building your path to wealth.

Remember, anyone can do it. It's not about having specialized skills or secret sauces. It's about understanding the system, making smart decisions, and taking action.

Chapter 1.3
Who can you be in this world?
Understanding Your Role in the Monetary System

Worker or Business Owner/Investor

One of the fundamental decisions you will make in your financial journey is whether to be a worker or a business owner/investor. This decision will shape your approach to the monetary system and ultimately determine your path to financial success.

As a worker, your primary role is to contribute your labour and skills to a business or organization in exchange for a salary or wages. This path offers stability and a predictable income, which can provide a sense of security. However, it often comes with limitations on how much you can earn and how fast you can grow your wealth. Your financial success in this role largely depends on your ability to increase your earning potential through promotions, additional education, or changing jobs.

On the other hand, becoming a business owner or investor shifts your role in the monetary system. As a business owner, you create value by providing goods or services, which can potentially yield higher financial rewards than being a worker. This path involves more risk but offers the opportunity for significant financial growth and independence. As an investor, you allocate capital into various ventures such as stocks, real estate, or startups, aiming to generate returns. This role allows you to leverage your money to work for you, creating passive income streams and compounding wealth over time.

Understanding these roles and the associated risks and rewards is crucial. By making an informed choice about whether to pursue a career as a worker or to take on the entrepreneurial and investor route, you can strategically plan your financial journey and maximize your potential for wealth creation and financial freedom.

The Basic Path: Being a Worker

Being a worker is the most straightforward way to engage with the monetary system. It's the path that most people choose because it offers immediate and stable income. Workers provide their labour in exchange for wages, which they use to cover their living expenses. This cycle of working for money is deeply ingrained in our society and is the basis of most people's financial strategy.

For many, the appeal of being a worker lies in the security and predictability it offers. A regular pay check ensures that basic needs such as housing, food, and healthcare are met. This stability allows workers to plan for their short-term and long-term goals, such as saving for a vacation, buying a home, or contributing to a retirement fund.

Moreover, the worker's path often includes opportunities for professional development and career advancement. By acquiring new skills, gaining experience, and possibly receiving promotions, workers can increase their earning potential over time. Many companies also provide benefits such as health insurance, retirement plans, and paid time off, which add to the overall compensation package and provide additional security.

However, while being a worker offers stability, it also has its limitations. The primary limitation is the cap on income; even with raises and promotions, there is a ceiling to how much one can earn solely through wages. Additionally, workers are typically trading time for money, meaning that their earning potential is directly tied to the hours they work.

Understanding the benefits and limitations of being a worker is essential. It allows individuals to make informed decisions about their careers and financial strategies, whether they choose to remain in the workforce or transition to becoming business owners or investors for greater financial growth and independence.

Different Types of Workers

Not all workers are the same. There are low-paying and high-paying workers, each with different levels of income and lifestyle.

Low-paying workers often occupy roles that require less specialized skills and education, such as retail workers, factory employees, and service industry staff. These jobs, while essential to the functioning of our economy, typically offer lower wages and fewer benefits. Workers in these roles might find it challenging to save money and invest for the future due to their limited financial resources. They often have to focus on meeting immediate needs, such as housing, food, and transportation, with little left over for savings or discretionary spending.

High-paying workers, on the other hand, have roles that require significant education, training, and experience. These positions include professions such as doctors, lawyers, engineers, and executives. The investment in education and training for these roles is substantial, often involving years of schooling and significant financial cost.

However, the return on this investment can be high, as these workers typically earn higher salaries and enjoy greater job stability and benefits. High-paying workers have more financial flexibility, allowing them to save, invest, and build wealth more effectively than their lower-paid counterparts.

Moreover, the difference in income levels between low-paying and high-paying workers also influences their lifestyle and financial goals. High-paying workers can afford a higher standard of living, access better healthcare, and provide more opportunities for their families. They are also better positioned to take advantage of financial opportunities such as investing in stocks, real estate, or retirement accounts.

Understanding these distinctions is crucial for anyone navigating their career path. It highlights the importance of education and skill development for those aiming to transition from low-paying to high-paying roles. It also underscores the diverse experiences and challenges faced by workers across different income levels, emphasizing the need for tailored financial strategies to achieve financial success and stability.

The Appeal of High-Paying Jobs

The allure of high-paying jobs is strong. Many people strive to attain these positions because they promise a higher income, which translates to a better lifestyle. With more money, individuals can afford larger homes, luxury cars, expensive clothing, and frequent travel. This desire for a higher standard of living drives many to pursue advanced education and training, hoping to land a lucrative job. High-paying jobs not only offer financial security but also provide a sense of achievement and social status. The ability to enjoy finer things in life, provide quality education for their children, and secure a comfortable retirement are significant motivators.

Moreover, high-paying jobs often come with additional perks such as comprehensive health benefits, retirement plans, stock options, and bonuses. These benefits add to the overall compensation package, making these positions even more attractive. The prestige associated with high-paying careers can also enhance one's professional reputation and open doors to further career opportunities.

The pursuit of high-paying jobs often involves significant effort and dedication. Individuals invest time and resources in obtaining advanced degrees, certifications, and specialized skills. They may also seek out continuous professional development to stay competitive in their field. The rigorous path to securing a high-paying job can be challenging, but the potential rewards make it a worthwhile endeavour for many.

Additionally, high-paying jobs can offer greater job satisfaction and fulfillment. Positions in fields such as medicine, law, engineering, and finance often involve challenging and impactful work, allowing individuals to make significant contributions to society. The combination of financial rewards, personal fulfillment, and social recognition makes high-paying jobs highly desirable. Consequently, many people are willing to put in the necessary work and sacrifices to achieve these coveted roles, aiming for a brighter and more prosperous future.

The Limitations of Being a Worker

However, even high-paying jobs come with limitations. Despite earning a substantial income, high earners often find themselves caught in a cycle of increased spending. They upgrade their lifestyles in proportion to their earnings, which can result in living pay check to pay check, albeit with a higher standard of living. This phenomenon is known as "lifestyle inflation." As their income rises, they tend to spend more on luxury items, dining out, and other non-essential expenses, leading to little or no savings. The pressure to maintain a certain social status and keep up with peers can further exacerbate this spending behaviour.

Moreover, being a worker, regardless of the pay, means trading time for money. This model inherently limits earning potential because there are only so many hours in a day. High-paying jobs often demand long hours, increased stress, and significant sacrifices in personal and family time. The risk of burnout and the lack of job security in some high-paying roles add to the limitations.

Another significant drawback is the dependency on a single source of income. If the job is lost due to economic downturns, corporate restructuring, or other unforeseen circumstances, the financial impact can be devastating. Workers have limited control over their financial futures and are vulnerable to changes in the job market and economy.

Furthermore, the pursuit of high-paying jobs often involves substantial student debt, especially in professions requiring advanced degrees. The burden of repaying these loans can offset the benefits of a high salary for many years. This debt can restrict financial freedom and delay other financial goals, such as buying a home or investing.

In summary, while high-paying jobs provide immediate financial rewards and a higher standard of living, they come with significant limitations. Lifestyle inflation, time constraints, job dependency, and potential debt can all hinder long-term financial stability and growth. Recognizing these limitations is crucial for anyone seeking to achieve true financial independence.

The Illusion of Wealth

Having more money and higher expenses does not equate to true wealth. It merely creates the illusion of wealth. True wealth is not just about earning a high income; it's about how you manage and grow your money. Many high earners fail to realize this and fall into the trap of spending all their earnings, leaving little room for savings and investments. This spending pattern leads to a precarious financial situation where, despite a substantial income, individuals have little to no financial security or future growth potential.

The illusion of wealth often manifests in the form of luxurious lifestyles: large homes, expensive cars, designer clothes, and frequent vacations. While these outward signs of affluence may impress others and provide short-term satisfaction, they do not contribute to long-term financial stability. In fact, they can lead to significant financial strain if not managed properly. High earners can become ensnared in a cycle of debt, using credit to maintain their lifestyles, which only exacerbates the illusion.

True wealth is built on a foundation of prudent financial management. This means living below your means, saving diligently, and investing wisely. It requires discipline and a shift in mindset from immediate gratification to long-term financial health. Wealthy individuals understand the power of compounding interest and the importance of having multiple streams of income. They focus on building assets that generate passive income, such as real estate, stocks, and businesses, which provide financial security and growth over time.

Moreover, true wealth is also about financial independence and the freedom to make choices without being constrained by financial limitations. It is the peace of mind that comes from knowing you have sufficient resources to handle emergencies and retire comfortably. By managing and growing your money wisely, you move beyond the illusion of wealth and achieve genuine, lasting financial success.

Chapter 1.4
The Smart Approach: Saving and Investing

The key to achieving financial independence and true wealth lies in the ability to save and invest wisely. This fundamental principle is the cornerstone of financial success and is the main message of this book. While many individuals focus solely on increasing their income, truly smart individuals understand that higher earnings alone are not enough to secure a prosperous financial future. Instead, they use their increased income as an opportunity to save more rather than spend more.

Smart individuals recognize that a disciplined approach to saving is the first step toward financial freedom. They understand that by consistently setting aside a portion of their income, they can build a solid financial foundation. This disciplined saving is not about deprivation but about prioritizing long-term goals over short-term gratification. By living below their means and avoiding lifestyle inflation, they create a financial buffer that can be used for investments.

Investing is the next critical step in the smart approach to financial management. Smart individuals know that merely saving money is not enough; they must also make their money work for them. By investing their savings in various assets, such as stocks, real estate, and businesses, they can generate additional income and grow their wealth over time. Investments have the potential to yield returns that far exceed the interest earned from traditional savings accounts, making them an essential component of wealth-building.

Moreover, smart investors understand the importance of diversification and risk management. They spread their investments across different asset classes to mitigate risk and maximize potential returns. They also stay informed about market trends and continuously educate themselves to make informed investment decisions.

The smart approach to saving and investing is not a get-rich-quick scheme but a systematic and disciplined method to build wealth over time. It requires patience, persistence, and a long-term perspective. By following this approach, anyone can achieve financial independence and true wealth, regardless of their starting point. This book will guide you through the principles and strategies of smart saving and investing, empowering you to take control of your financial future and achieve your dreams.

Steps to Financial Independence

Save a Portion of Your Income: Regardless of your income level, it's essential to save a portion of your earnings consistently. This practice is the cornerstone of financial independence, as it creates a financial cushion and provides capital for future investments. Start by setting aside a fixed percentage of your income each month. Automating this process can make it easier to maintain discipline. Over time, your savings will grow, giving you the financial stability to weather unexpected expenses and the flexibility to seize investment opportunities. Additionally, building an emergency fund that covers at least three to six months' worth of living expenses is a crucial part of this step. This fund acts as a safety net, ensuring that you won't have to dip into your investments in case of an unforeseen financial setback.

Invest Wisely: Investing your savings can help grow your wealth exponentially. There are various investment avenues to consider, such as the stock market, real estate, or starting your own business. Each option comes with its own set of risks and rewards, and it's crucial to conduct thorough research before making any decisions. In the stock market, for example, understanding the fundamentals of the companies you invest in and diversifying your portfolio can mitigate risks. Real estate investments require knowledge of market trends, property valuation, and management. Starting a business involves careful planning, market research, and a solid business plan. Regardless of the chosen investment, staying informed and continuously educating yourself is key to making wise investment choices. It's also beneficial to seek advice from financial advisors or mentors who have experience in your chosen investment field.

Reinvest Profits: Instead of spending the returns from your investments, reinvest them to compound your wealth further. This strategy leverages the power of compound interest, where your investment earnings generate additional earnings. For instance, if you invest in dividend-paying stocks, reinvesting the dividends can significantly increase your overall returns over time. Similarly, in real estate, reinvesting rental income into additional properties can expand your portfolio and increase your passive income streams. This reinvestment approach accelerates your journey to financial independence by allowing your wealth to grow at an increasingly rapid rate. Maintaining a long-term perspective and avoiding the temptation to withdraw your investment returns prematurely is essential for maximizing the benefits of compound growth.

By following these steps diligently, you can build a solid foundation for financial independence. Saving consistently, making informed investment decisions, and reinvesting profits create a powerful cycle of wealth accumulation. This disciplined approach requires patience and persistence, but over time, it can transform your financial situation, providing you with the freedom and security to achieve your life goals.

Chapter 1.5
Beyond Being a Worker

While being a worker is a simple and common way to engage with the monetary system, becoming a business owner or investor offers greater potential for wealth creation and financial independence. As a business owner, you can generate multiple income streams, scale your operations, and leverage resources to maximize profits. As an investor, you can benefit from the growth and success of businesses without being directly involved in day-to-day operations. Both paths allow you to take control of your financial future, build significant wealth, and achieve a level of financial freedom that is often unattainable through traditional employment alone.

The Role of a Business Owner/Investor

A business owner or investor uses their capital to generate income through business ventures or investments. This role involves a different set of skills and a higher level of risk compared to being a worker, but it also offers the potential for higher rewards. As a business owner, you have the opportunity to create and control an enterprise that can grow and scale, generating profits beyond the limitations of a fixed salary. You must possess or develop skills in leadership, strategic planning, and financial management to effectively run a business. Understanding market dynamics, identifying opportunities, and making informed decisions are crucial to success.

Investors, on the other hand, allocate their capital to various investment vehicles such as stocks, bonds, real estate, or other businesses. This requires a deep understanding of financial markets, risk assessment, and investment strategies. Successful investors are adept at analysing potential investments, diversifying their portfolios to mitigate risks, and staying informed about economic trends and market conditions. The ability to evaluate the financial health of companies, project future growth, and recognize undervalued assets is essential.

Both business owners and investors must be comfortable with uncertainty and capable of making decisions under pressure. The higher level of risk associated with these roles is counterbalanced by the potential for substantial financial gains. Unlike a worker, whose income is typically limited to wages or a salary, business owners and investors can experience exponential growth in their wealth through the appreciation of assets, profit reinvestment, and leveraging capital.

Additionally, being a business owner or investor provides the flexibility and autonomy to make strategic choices that align with personal financial goals. This path also enables the creation of passive income streams, offering a pathway to financial independence and long-term security. While the journey requires dedication, continuous learning, and resilience, the rewards of being a business owner or investor can be significantly more fulfilling and lucrative than traditional employment.

Making the Transition

Transitioning from being a worker to a business owner or investor involves a significant mindset shift and a readiness to embrace calculated risks. This change is not just about altering your professional role but about fundamentally rethinking your approach to money and growth. Here are some critical steps to consider as you embark on this journey:

Educate Yourself: The first step is to gain a comprehensive understanding of the various investment opportunities and business ventures available. Educate yourself about the stock market, real estate, startups, and other asset classes. Understand the inherent risks and potential rewards associated with each option. This might involve reading books, taking online courses, attending seminars, or following industry news. The more informed you are, the better equipped you'll be to make strategic decisions that align with your financial goals.

Start Small: Rather than jumping in with significant investments or launching a large-scale business immediately, begin with smaller, manageable projects.

This could mean investing a modest amount in the stock market, starting a side business, or dabbling in real estate. Starting small allows you to gain hands-on experience, understand market dynamics, and build confidence without risking substantial amounts of capital. It also helps in developing a realistic perspective on what it takes to succeed in business and investing.

<u>Network</u>: Building connections with experienced business owners and investors is invaluable. Networking offers insights that can't be found in textbooks or online resources. Attend industry events, join professional organizations, and seek out mentorship from those who have navigated the path before you. Learning from their successes and failures can provide guidance and help you avoid common pitfalls. Networking also opens doors to potential partnerships and investment opportunities.

<u>Stay Committed</u>: The journey to becoming a successful business owner or investor requires dedication and resilience. Financial growth through these avenues is often gradual and can come with setbacks. Stay committed to your goals, continuously refine your strategies, and be prepared to adapt based on what you learn from your experiences. Embrace failures as learning opportunities and use them to improve your approach. Remember, long-term success is built on perseverance, continual learning, and adaptability.

By following these steps, you can effectively make the transition from being a worker to becoming a business owner or investor, positioning yourself for greater financial growth and independence.

Understanding your role in the monetary system is essential for making informed and strategic financial decisions. The traditional path of being a worker offers a stable and predictable source of income. For many, this is the most familiar and accessible way to engage with the economy. Workers receive wages in exchange for their labour, which provides a dependable financial foundation. However, while this stability is valuable, it often imposes limitations on wealth creation. The cycle of earning wages and covering expenses can lead to a comfortable lifestyle but rarely allows for significant financial growth beyond a certain point.

In contrast, transitioning from being solely a worker to becoming a business owner or investor opens up greater possibilities for financial independence and wealth accumulation. Business owners and investors use their capital to create and grow assets, which can lead to substantial financial returns. This shift involves a different set of skills, including risk management, strategic planning, and market analysis. Although the risks are higher compared to traditional employment, the potential rewards can be significantly greater.

This book is designed to guide you through the transition from being a worker to becoming a business owner or investor. It provides a comprehensive roadmap, including practical steps and strategies to help you make informed decisions and maximize your financial potential. Whether you are starting with a modest income or aiming to enhance your existing financial portfolio, the principles outlined here can help you build and sustain wealth over time.

Remember, true wealth is not solely determined by how much you earn, but by how effectively you manage and grow your money. By applying the strategies discussed in this book, you can unlock your full financial potential and achieve independence. Let's embark on this journey together, transforming your financial future and realizing your wealth-building goals.

Chapter 1.6
Becoming a Business Owner

Starting a business is often viewed as a pivotal step towards financial independence and wealth creation. The idea of being your own boss and enjoying the profits from your enterprise can be incredibly appealing. However, many entrepreneurs quickly discover that starting a business often leads them into the trenches of daily operations, where they find themselves managing every aspect of their business, from customer service to inventory management. This active involvement can consume a significant amount of time and energy, leaving little room for other pursuits or personal freedom.

To truly achieve financial independence through business ownership, it's crucial to transition from being an active manager to a passive owner. This transition involves several strategic steps.

First, focus on building a solid business foundation with efficient systems and processes. Implementing robust operational procedures and investing in technology can help streamline day-to-day tasks and reduce the need for constant oversight.

Second, delegate responsibilities effectively. Hiring competent staff or managers who can handle routine operations allows you to step back from daily involvement. This not only frees up your time but also ensures that your business continues to run smoothly in your absence. Empower your team with the authority and resources they need to make decisions and manage operations independently.

Third, consider creating or acquiring passive income streams within your business. For example, you could develop products or services that generate recurring revenue with minimal ongoing effort, such as subscription-based services or automated online sales platforms.

Additionally, it's important to maintain oversight and strategic involvement without micromanaging. Regularly reviewing key performance indicators and financial reports allows you to stay informed about your business's health and make strategic adjustments as needed.

Ultimately, transitioning from an active management role to a passive ownership role in your business requires thoughtful planning, effective delegation, and strategic investment in systems and processes. By focusing on these areas, you can enjoy the financial rewards of your business while reclaiming your time and achieving greater financial freedom.

The Challenge of Starting a Small Business

Starting a small business often begins as an exciting yet daunting endeavour. In the initial stages, you, as the entrepreneur, are typically required to wear multiple hats. You're not just the owner; you become the manager, marketer, salesperson, and even the accountant. This hands-on involvement is essential for getting the business off the ground. The early days are marked by long hours and significant personal investment, both financially and emotionally. This active participation is crucial for setting up the foundational aspects of the business, such as developing a business plan, securing funding, and establishing a customer base.

However, this multifaceted role can quickly become a double-edged sword. While your engagement is vital for initial success, it also means that you've effectively created a job for yourself. The responsibilities of running a small business can be overwhelming. From managing daily operations and handling customer inquiries to overseeing inventory and ensuring compliance with regulations, the range of tasks can be extensive. This intensive involvement often leaves little time for strategic planning or personal relaxation.

Moreover, this hands-on approach can blur the lines between investment and active management. Instead of simply investing capital and reaping the benefits, you become deeply entrenched in the operational aspects of the business. This shift can be challenging, as it demands a high level of commitment and can lead to burnout if not managed effectively. Balancing the immediate demands of running the business with long-term strategic goals requires careful planning and effective time management.

Over time, the challenge of starting a small business lies in transitioning from this initial phase of intense personal involvement to a more sustainable model. This involves building systems and delegating tasks to others, so you can step back from daily operations and focus on strategic growth. Understanding this challenge is crucial for long-term success and achieving the desired balance between involvement and passive ownership.

Example: The Common Small Business Owner Scenario

Imagine you start a small bakery. You love baking, and you're passionate about bringing delicious pastries to your community. In the beginning, you're involved in every aspect of the business: baking, customer service, bookkeeping, marketing, and supply chain management. Your bakery becomes successful, but you're working long hours, and your income depends on your constant presence and effort. You've created a profitable business, but you're also tied to it.

The Transition to Passive Ownership

Starting a business often requires an intense level of personal involvement, with the founder taking on multiple roles—manager, marketer, salesperson, and more. This hands-on approach is essential for establishing the business and navigating its early challenges. However, as the business grows, the ultimate goal should be to transition from being an active manager to assuming a passive ownership role. This transition allows you to benefit from the business's profits without being consumed by its daily operations.

The first step in transitioning to passive ownership is to create robust systems and processes. This involves streamlining operations so that the business can function efficiently with minimal oversight. Establishing clear procedures, delegating responsibilities, and implementing effective management structures are critical components. By automating routine tasks and empowering a competent team, you can reduce your day-to-day involvement. Investing in technology and software that enhance operational efficiency can also facilitate this shift.

Another strategy for achieving passive ownership is to focus on building a strong, reliable management team. Hiring experienced managers who share your vision and values can ensure that the business continues to operate smoothly in your absence. Providing them with the tools and authority to make decisions will be key to maintaining operational continuity.

Alternatively, purchasing an existing profitable business can be an effective way to achieve passive ownership more quickly. By acquiring a business with a proven track record and established systems, you can bypass many of the initial challenges of starting from scratch. This approach allows you to benefit from the business's existing infrastructure and revenue streams while focusing on strategic growth rather than daily management.

Ultimately, the transition to passive ownership involves balancing your role between overseeing strategic direction and allowing the business to operate independently. This shift can lead to greater financial freedom and enable you to pursue other interests or investments while continuing to enjoy the benefits of business ownership.

Chapter 1.7
Embracing Passive Ownership

Transitioning from an active managerial role to passive ownership represents a pivotal step toward achieving true financial freedom. This shift allows you to benefit from the financial success of your business without being bogged down by its daily operational demands. By embracing passive ownership, you open the door to a lifestyle enriched by personal fulfillment, quality family time, and leisure activities, all while continuing to enjoy the financial rewards of your business investments.

Passive ownership enables you to enjoy the financial fruits of your labour without being constantly involved in the intricacies of daily management. This newfound freedom allows you to focus on what truly matters to you—whether it's spending more time with loved ones, pursuing personal interests, or simply enjoying a well-deserved break. It offers a chance to reallocate your time and energy towards activities that enhance your overall quality of life, rather than being tied to the routine challenges of managing a business.

One strategic approach to achieving passive ownership is by acquiring existing successful businesses. Purchasing a business with a proven track record and well-established systems allows you to bypass many of the initial hurdles of starting a business from scratch. This method provides a more immediate path to passive income, as you can benefit from the business's existing operations and revenue streams while refining and optimizing its performance.

Additionally, the stock market offers another compelling avenue for passive income. Investing in dividend-paying stocks, index funds, or mutual funds can generate a steady stream of income with minimal day-to-day involvement. By diversifying your investments and focusing on long-term growth, you can build a portfolio that provides consistent returns and complements your journey toward financial freedom.

Ultimately, embracing passive ownership means adopting a strategic mindset that values long-term gains over immediate involvement. It's about creating a sustainable income stream that supports your desired lifestyle while allowing you to step back from the everyday demands of business management. This path to financial freedom not only enhances your financial well-being but also enriches your life, providing the space and resources to pursue your passions and enjoy a more balanced existence.

The Appeal of Passive Ownership

Passive ownership represents the pinnacle of financial independence for those who seek to reap the benefits of their investments without being ensnared in the daily grind of business operations. At its core, passive ownership means you, as a business owner or investor, can step back from the constant demands of managing a business while still enjoying its financial rewards. This approach allows you to invest in a well-established system or enterprise that generates income on its own, freeing you from the need to be perpetually involved in its day-to-day activities.

The allure of passive ownership lies in its ability to provide a steady stream of income while allowing you to redirect your focus toward other significant aspects of life. Whether it's spending quality time with family, indulging in personal hobbies, or exploring new destinations through travel, passive ownership grants you the freedom to live a more balanced and fulfilling life.

By creating or acquiring a business model that operates efficiently without your constant oversight, you can achieve a sense of financial security and personal freedom. This transition not only enhances your financial stability but also enriches your overall quality of life, enabling you to pursue your passions and enjoy experiences that contribute to a more rewarding and enjoyable existence.

Example: The Passive Owner's Lifestyle

Imagine owning a chain of laundromats. Instead of managing each location, you hire competent managers and staff to handle the operations. Your role is limited to overseeing the business from a higher level, making strategic decisions, and occasionally checking in to ensure everything runs smoothly. The laundromats generate consistent income, and you enjoy the freedom to live life on your terms.

The Advantages of Buying an Existing Successful Business

Purchasing an existing successful business is a strategic and efficient route to achieving financial independence and passive ownership. Unlike starting a business from scratch, which is often fraught with uncertainties, a steep learning curve, and numerous challenges, acquiring an established business provides several distinct advantages that can significantly enhance your path to success.

One of the most compelling reasons to purchase an established business is the benefit of a proven track record. An existing business comes with a detailed history of financial performance, including revenue trends, profitability, and operational efficiency. This historical data allows potential buyers to make well-informed decisions by assessing the business's stability and growth potential. Instead of navigating unknowns, as one would with a new venture, acquiring a business with a clear picture of past performance reduces the risks associated with investment. The track record of the business provides valuable insights into its profitability, market position, and operational efficiency, thereby minimizing the guesswork typically associated with new ventures.

Another significant advantage of buying an existing business is the presence of an established customer base. This loyal clientele is already familiar with the business and its offerings, ensuring a steady stream of revenue from the outset. The existence of a strong customer base means that you can build on existing relationships rather than starting from scratch, which significantly accelerates the path to profitability. The time and effort required to attract new customers are considerably reduced, allowing you to focus on maintaining and enhancing these relationships, which is crucial for sustained growth.

Operational systems are another crucial aspect where existing businesses have the upper hand. Established businesses have refined their processes over time, including inventory management, supply chain logistics, employee procedures, and marketing strategies. These systems are typically well-documented and functioning smoothly, allowing you to step in as an owner without the need to overhaul the operational framework. The streamlined processes ensure smooth operations with minimal disruption, reducing the need for hands-on management and enabling you to concentrate on strategic improvements rather than everyday operational issues.

Furthermore, purchasing a successful business often means inheriting a motivated and experienced team. This team has likely been instrumental in the business's success, and their continued involvement can ensure a smooth transition and ongoing operational excellence. The experience and expertise of the existing staff are invaluable assets that contribute to the business's sustained performance, further reducing the risks associated with the acquisition.

Brand recognition is another significant advantage of buying an existing business. A well-known business comes with an established reputation and market presence, which can be leveraged to drive continued success. The brand's established credibility and customer trust provide a competitive edge, making it easier to attract and retain customers. This brand value not only enhances the immediate appeal of the business but also provides a solid foundation for future growth and expansion.

In summary, acquiring an existing successful business offers numerous advantages, including a proven track record, an established customer base, efficient operational systems, an experienced team, and valuable brand recognition. These benefits not only mitigate many of the risks associated with starting a new business but also set the stage for a successful and profitable venture. For those looking to transition to passive ownership and secure long-term financial success, purchasing an existing business is a strategic and rewarding choice.

Example: Buying a Profitable Restaurant

Consider purchasing a popular restaurant with a loyal customer base and positive cash flow. The restaurant has been operating successfully for years, and its systems and staff are well-established. As the new owner, you step in and oversee the business strategically, but the day-to-day operations are handled by experienced managers. You enjoy the profits without the stress of starting from scratch or managing every detail.

Chapter 1.8
The Allure of the Stock Market

The stock market represents one of the most accessible and appealing ways to achieve passive ownership and build wealth with minimal hands-on involvement. When you invest in the stock market, you purchase shares of publicly traded companies, thereby becoming a partial owner of those businesses. This investment strategy offers several compelling advantages that make it a popular choice for achieving financial growth.

One of the primary attractions of the stock market is the opportunity for passive income. As a shareholder, you can benefit from dividends, which are periodic payments made to shareholders from a company's earnings. Dividends provide a steady stream of income without requiring active participation in the company's operations. Additionally, you can realize capital gains when the value of your shares appreciates over time. As the stock price increases, the value of your investment grows, allowing you to sell shares at a profit.

Investing in the stock market also provides the advantage of diversification. By holding shares in multiple companies across various sectors, you spread your investment risk and reduce the impact of any single company's poor performance on your overall portfolio. This diversification helps to stabilize returns and minimizes the potential for significant losses.

Another appealing aspect of stock market investing is the relatively low barrier to entry. Unlike starting a business or acquiring real estate, investing in stocks requires a lower initial capital investment and can be done through online brokerage accounts with minimal fees. This accessibility allows investors of varying financial backgrounds to participate and benefit from the market.

Furthermore, stock market investments are typically more liquid compared to other forms of investments like real estate or private businesses. This liquidity means that you can easily buy or sell shares, making it simpler to adjust your investment strategy as needed.

In summary, the stock market offers an attractive route to passive ownership, enabling you to participate in the financial success of various companies without the need for direct involvement in their operations. With the potential for dividends, capital gains, diversification, and liquidity, investing in the stock market can be a powerful tool for building wealth and achieving financial independence.

Advantages of Stock Market Investments:

Investing in the stock market offers several compelling advantages that make it an attractive option for those seeking to build wealth and achieve financial goals. Understanding these benefits can help you make informed decisions about how to allocate your investment capital effectively.

Ease of Entry: One of the most significant advantages of stock market investments is the ease with which you can get started. Buying stocks is a straightforward process that can be completed with just a few clicks online through a brokerage account. Unlike starting or purchasing a business, which involves complex legal, financial, and operational considerations, investing in stocks is accessible and requires minimal setup. This simplicity allows investors to begin building their portfolios with relative ease and efficiency.

Diversification: The stock market provides a unique opportunity to diversify your investments across a wide range of industries and companies. Diversification involves spreading your investments across different assets to reduce risk and enhance potential returns. By holding shares in various sectors, you mitigate the impact of poor performance in any single area, thereby stabilizing your overall portfolio. This approach helps manage risk and can lead to more consistent returns over time.

Liquidity: Stocks are known for their high liquidity, meaning that they can be bought and sold quickly in the market. This liquidity is a significant advantage because it allows you to access your money with relative ease if you need to make withdrawals or adjust your investment strategy. The ability to enter and exit positions swiftly provides flexibility and control over your investments, making it easier to respond to market changes or personal financial needs.

<u>Professional Management</u>: Investing in stocks also means that you benefit from the expertise of professional management teams. Publicly traded companies are managed by experienced executives who work diligently to maximize shareholder value and drive growth. Additionally, many companies distribute dividends to their shareholders, providing a regular income stream without requiring any additional effort on your part. This combination of professional oversight and passive income can contribute to a well-rounded investment strategy.

The stock market offers a range of advantages, including ease of entry, diversification, liquidity, and the benefits of professional management. These features make stock market investments a powerful tool for building wealth and achieving financial independence. By leveraging these advantages, investors can work towards their financial goals with greater confidence and efficiency.

<u>Example: Investing in a Tech Giant</u>
Imagine investing in a leading technology company by purchasing its shares. You become a part-owner of a globally recognized business that innovates and grows continuously. The company's management team handles all the operations, product development, and market strategies. Your role is simply to hold the shares and benefit from the company's success through dividends and stock price appreciation.

The Drawbacks of Stock Market Investments

While the stock market offers numerous advantages for passive investors, it is crucial to be mindful of its potential drawbacks to make informed investment decisions. Understanding these limitations can help you navigate the market more effectively and manage your expectations.

Market Volatility: One of the most significant drawbacks of investing in the stock market is its inherent volatility. Stock prices can experience substantial fluctuations due to a variety of factors, including changes in market conditions, economic indicators, and company performance. This volatility can impact the value of your investments, causing short-term losses even if the long-term outlook remains positive. For investors who are uncomfortable with the potential for rapid and unpredictable changes in their portfolio value, market volatility can be a considerable concern.

Lack of Control: As a shareholder, you have limited control over a company's operations and strategic decisions. Your role is primarily that of a passive investor, and you rely on the company's management team to make decisions that will drive the company's success and, consequently, the performance of your investment. This lack of control can be frustrating, especially if the company's management makes decisions that you disagree with or that negatively impact the stock's performance.

Dividends Are Not Guaranteed: While many companies pay dividends to shareholders, these payments are not guaranteed. Companies may reduce or eliminate their dividend payments during periods of financial difficulty or economic downturns. This can affect your income stream, particularly if you rely on dividends as a primary source of income. It is essential to be prepared for the possibility that dividend payments may fluctuate or be discontinued altogether.

Market Timing: Attempting to time the market—buying stocks at their lowest price and selling them at their highest—can be incredibly challenging. Even experienced investors often struggle with market timing, leading to suboptimal results and missed opportunities. Attempting to predict market movements with precision can result in emotional decision-making and potential losses.

Despite these drawbacks, the stock market remains a powerful tool for passive income and wealth creation when approached with a long-term perspective and a diversified strategy. By understanding and managing these limitations, investors can harness the benefits of stock market investments while mitigating potential risks.

Chapter 1.9
The Goal: Passive Income and Financial Independence

The pursuit of passive income represents a transformative step toward achieving financial independence and redefining your lifestyle. Passive income, by its nature, is money earned with minimal ongoing effort or direct involvement, allowing you to build wealth while freeing up your time for personal pursuits and interests. The ultimate objective is to generate a steady stream of income that covers your living expenses, enabling you to live life on your own terms and pursue your passions without the constraints of a traditional work schedule.

One of the primary ways to achieve passive income is through the acquisition of an existing successful business. By purchasing a well-established company with a proven track record, you can benefit from its established revenue streams, customer base, and operational systems. This approach reduces the initial risks and uncertainties associated with starting a new business from scratch. An effective strategy involves not just buying a business, but also setting it up in a way that allows you to step back from daily operations. Delegating management responsibilities and optimizing operational efficiency are crucial for ensuring that the business continues to generate income without requiring constant hands-on involvement from you.

Alternatively, investing in the stock market offers another viable route to passive income. By purchasing shares of publicly traded companies, you become a partial owner and can benefit from dividends and capital gains. The stock market provides opportunities for diversification, allowing you to spread your investments across various industries and companies to manage risk while aiming for growth. Many investors focus on acquiring dividend-paying stocks that offer regular income distributions. However, it's important to maintain a long-term perspective and avoid attempting to time the market, as short-term fluctuations can impact returns.

Both paths to passive income—buying an established business or investing in the stock market—require careful planning, research, and strategic execution. Key steps include assessing potential investments, understanding market dynamics, and continuously monitoring performance to ensure alignment with your financial goals. By achieving a steady flow of passive income, you can attain financial independence, allowing you to allocate your time and resources according to your personal aspirations and desires.

Ultimately, the goal is to create a financial ecosystem that supports your lifestyle choices and provides you with the freedom to enjoy life without being constrained by the necessity of active employment. Embracing passive ownership and income strategies paves the way to a more flexible, rewarding, and fulfilling life.

Key Takeaways:

Passive Ownership: The essence of passive ownership lies in selecting investments that generate income without demanding your constant involvement. This approach allows you to benefit from the profits of your investments while avoiding the daily responsibilities and time commitments typically associated with active management. By focusing on assets or opportunities that provide ongoing revenue streams with minimal effort on your part, you can create a more relaxed and manageable financial strategy.

Buy Existing Businesses: Acquiring established businesses can be a highly effective method for achieving passive income. Opt for businesses with a proven track record of success and stability. These businesses come with an existing customer base, established operational systems, and a history of financial performance, which can significantly reduce the risks and uncertainties associated with starting a new venture. When you purchase a well-run business, you inherit its success and can often enjoy a smoother transition to passive income, as the groundwork has already been laid.

<u>Stock Market Investments</u>: The stock market offers a powerful tool for building wealth with relatively minimal effort. By investing in stocks, particularly those that pay dividends, you can create a diversified portfolio that generates on-going income. Diversification across different industries and companies helps manage risk and enhance potential returns. With the right strategy and long-term perspective, stock market investments can grow your wealth and provide a steady stream of passive income.

<u>Enjoy Life</u>: Financial independence is the ultimate goal of passive ownership. Achieving this level of financial stability means you can spend more time with your loved ones, engage in hobbies, and pursue a fulfilling lifestyle without the constraints of a traditional job. By strategically investing and managing your assets, you can secure a future where your financial resources support the life you envision, providing you with greater freedom and personal satisfaction.

Understanding and leveraging the principles of passive ownership allows you to build a secure financial future. The key is to invest wisely and strategically, ensuring that your money works for you while you enjoy the benefits of financial independence. By focusing on passive income streams, acquiring successful businesses, and utilizing stock market investments, you can achieve the freedom to live life on your own terms and fully embrace the opportunities that come your way.

Chapter 1.10
The Ultimate Guide to Financial Freedom: Save, Invest, and Achieve Passive Income

The path to financial independence and wealth is often seen as complex and unattainable by many. However, the core principles that lead to financial success are straightforward: save diligently, invest wisely, and focus on generating passive income. This guidebook aims to simplify these concepts and provide you with a clear, actionable roadmap to achieve your financial goals. The essence of this book is to teach you how to maximize your savings regardless of your income level, minimize unnecessary expenses, and invest in ways that generate passive income rather than requiring you to be an active manager of your investments.

The Foundation: Saving Money

The cornerstone of financial freedom starts with saving money. Savings are the building blocks of your financial future, and your ability to save is directly influenced by two main factors: your income and your expenses.

1. Understanding Your Income:

Your income is largely determined by the occupation you choose. Different professions have varying pay scales and career trajectories. For example, someone who completes a three-year training program to become a plumber can start earning a good income by age 20. In contrast, a person studying to become a doctor may not start earning until their late twenties or early thirties, albeit at a higher income level.

The key takeaway is that the sooner you start earning, the sooner you can start saving and investing. It's important to choose an occupation that not only aligns with your interests and skills but also offers a balance between the time spent in education and the potential income.

2. Managing Your Expenses:

No matter how much you earn, your ability to save depends on how well you manage your expenses. High earners can still find themselves in financial trouble if their spending habits are out of control. Conversely, individuals with modest incomes can accumulate significant savings by being frugal and making smart financial choices.

To maximize your savings, consider the following strategies:

- **Living Arrangements:** If possible, live with your parents or share accommodation to reduce rent costs.
- **Minimalist Lifestyle:** Avoid buying expensive clothing and gadgets. Focus on essentials.
- **Home-Cooked Meals:** Eating out frequently can drain your finances. Learn to cook and prepare meals at home.
- **Transportation:** Buy used vehicles instead of new ones. A reliable, inexpensive car can save you a lot of money.
- **Travel:** Instead of expensive international trips, opt for budget-friendly local travel and camping.

By making conscious choices about your lifestyle and spending habits, you can significantly increase the amount you save each month.

The Power of Investing

Once you have a solid foundation of savings, the next step is to invest your money. Investing is crucial because it allows your money to grow over time, leveraging the power of compound interest and market growth.

1. Choosing the Right Investments:

Investing can seem daunting, but it's important to understand that not all investments are created equal. The goal is to invest in assets that provide passive income, meaning you earn money without actively managing the investment on a daily basis.

Here are some popular types of investments that can generate passive income:

- **Real Estate:** Investing in rental properties can provide a steady stream of income. While there is some initial management required, you can hire property managers to handle the day-to-day operations.
- **Stocks:** Buying shares in established companies can yield dividends, which are regular payments made to shareholders. The stock market also offers the potential for capital appreciation, meaning the value of your shares can increase over time.
- **Bonds:** These are essentially loans you give to corporations or governments, which pay you interest over time. Bonds are generally lower risk compared to stocks.
- **Mutual Funds and ETFs:** These are collections of stocks and bonds managed by financial professionals. They offer diversification and can provide steady returns.

2. Emphasizing Passive Income:

The major appeal of passive income is that it allows you to earn money with minimal effort. Unlike a traditional job, where you trade time for money, passive income works for you around the clock. This gives you the freedom to spend your time on activities you enjoy, whether it's spending time with family, traveling, or pursuing hobbies.

The stock market is a prime example of how you can become a passive investor. By purchasing shares in publicly listed companies, you become a part-owner of the business. This means you share in the company's profits without having to manage the business operations. However, it's important to diversify your investments to spread risk and maximize returns.

The Goal: Financial Independence

The ultimate goal of saving and investing is to achieve financial independence. This means having enough passive income to cover your living expenses, allowing you to live comfortably without relying on a traditional job.

1. The Path to Financial Independence:

Achieving financial independence requires discipline and a long-term perspective. It's about making smart financial choices consistently over time. Here's a simplified roadmap:

- **Start Early:** The sooner you start saving and investing, the more time your money has to grow.
- **Be Consistent:** Make saving and investing a habit. Automate contributions to your investment accounts.
- **Educate Yourself:** Continuously learn about different investment options and strategies.
- **Stay the Course:** Markets fluctuate, but it's important to stay committed to your investment plan.

2. Enjoying the Benefits:

Once you reach financial independence, you have the freedom to make choices based on your desires rather than financial necessity. You can retire early, travel the world, pursue passion projects, or spend more time with loved ones. The peace of mind that comes from financial security is invaluable.

Conclusion

This guidebook is designed to provide you with the knowledge and tools to achieve financial success. By focusing on saving money, minimizing expenses, and investing in assets that generate passive income, you can build a solid financial foundation and work towards financial independence. Remember, the journey to wealth is not about having extraordinary skills or luck; it's about making informed decisions, starting early, and staying committed to your financial goals.

By adopting these principles and strategies, you can transform your financial future and live a life of abundance and freedom. Let this book be your companion on the path to financial success, helping you navigate the complexities of the financial world with confidence and clarity.

PART 2.
WEALTH BUILDING TOOLS

Chapter 2.1
BASICS OF SAVING

Savings is the cornerstone of financial success. Consistently saving money enables you to invest, grow wealth, and eventually achieve financial independence. Savings depend on two key factors: your income and your expenses. Understanding and managing these elements is crucial for building a strong financial foundation.

Maximizing your income potential is the first step. Whether through higher-paying job opportunities, developing new skills, or taking on additional work, every bit of extra income can significantly boost your savings.

Next, controlling your expenses is essential. Regardless of how much you earn, unchecked spending habits can undermine your ability to save. Create a detailed budget to track all income and expenditures, and identify areas where you can cut back, such as dining out or unnecessary subscriptions. Small adjustments can lead to substantial savings over time.

Adopting a frugal mindset further amplifies savings efforts. Look for ways to reduce costs without sacrificing quality of life, like cooking at home, using public transportation, or shopping during sales. Making thoughtful spending choices is key.

Setting clear, achievable savings goals provides motivation and direction. Consider automating your savings by setting up regular transfers to a dedicated savings account. This ensures a portion of your income is consistently set aside.

By effectively managing your income and expenses, embracing a frugal mindset, and setting clear savings goals, you can build a robust financial cushion. This disciplined approach to savings will empower you to invest wisely, grow your wealth, and ultimately achieve financial independence.

The Role of Income

Your income plays a pivotal role in shaping your financial future. The occupation you choose directly influences your earning potential, and this potential can vary widely across different professions. For instance, careers in technology, finance, and healthcare often offer higher salaries compared to roles in retail, hospitality, or manual labour. Furthermore, the time it takes to reach a significant income level can differ significantly. Professions requiring advanced degrees or specialized training, such as doctors, lawyers, and engineers, typically involve a longer educational pathway before substantial earnings begin.

However, it's not just about the occupation itself but also about the strategic choices you make within that field. Pursuing additional certifications, gaining specialized skills, or seeking promotions can enhance your earning potential over time. Networking and staying updated with industry trends can also open doors to higher-paying opportunities.

Geographic location is another crucial factor affecting income. Salaries can vary dramatically depending on the cost of living and demand for certain skills in different regions or countries. Urban areas with a high concentration of industries often offer higher wages compared to rural settings.

Additionally, the rise of the gig economy and remote work has introduced new avenues for income generation. Freelancing, consulting, and online businesses provide flexible opportunities to supplement traditional employment income or even replace it entirely.

Understanding the role of income in your financial strategy is essential. By carefully selecting your occupation, continually enhancing your skills, and exploring various income streams, you can maximize your earning potential. This strategic approach to managing your income will provide a strong foundation for achieving your financial goals and securing a prosperous future.

Choosing an Occupation:

When choosing an occupation, it's essential to consider both the training period and the potential income. This decision significantly influences your ability to save and invest over time, impacting your overall financial strategy.

1. Skilled Trades

    Skilled trades, such as plumbing, electrical work, and carpentry, often require shorter training periods compared to professional careers. Typically, an apprenticeship in these fields lasts around three years. For instance, a plumber can start earning a good income by the age of 20. This early start provides a significant advantage: more years to accumulate savings and make investments, leveraging the power of compound interest. Additionally, skilled trades offer job stability and high demand, often leading to lucrative and consistent work opportunities. By starting early in a skilled trade, individuals can build a robust financial foundation while potentially avoiding the significant student debt associated with longer educational pathways.

2. Professional Careers

    In contrast, professional careers such as medicine, law, or engineering require extensive education and training. A medical doctor, for example, might not start earning a substantial income until their late 20s or early 30s due to the lengthy period of undergraduate education, medical school, and residency. While the earning potential in these fields is typically very high, the delayed start can impact the early accumulation of savings and investments. The cost of education, including tuition fees and potential student loans, can also pose a financial burden initially. However, the long-term financial benefits often outweigh these early disadvantages. Professionals in these careers generally enjoy high salaries, which can facilitate rapid debt repayment and significant wealth accumulation once they start earning.

    Choosing an occupation requires balancing the duration and cost of education against the potential long-term income. Skilled trades offer the benefit of an early start in the workforce and the potential for steady, high-demand employment. In contrast, professional careers promise high salaries but require a substantial upfront investment of time and money. Understanding these dynamics can help you make an informed decision that aligns with your financial goals and personal interests. By strategically planning your career path, you can maximize your earning potential and set the stage for long-term financial success.

Income Levels

High-Paying Jobs: High-paying jobs, such as doctors, lawyers, engineers, and senior managers, offer substantial salaries that provide significant opportunities for saving and investing. For example, a senior manager or engineer might earn a six-figure salary, enabling them to save large sums of money and make substantial investments. The higher income levels associated with these professions can also facilitate a more comfortable lifestyle, allowing for discretionary spending without compromising savings goals. Additionally, the financial stability provided by high-paying jobs can support long-term investment strategies, including real estate, stocks, and retirement accounts, potentially leading to substantial wealth accumulation over time. The ability to invest larger amounts consistently can significantly impact the growth of one's wealth due to the power of compounding returns.

Moderate-Paying Jobs: Occupations such as teachers, nurses, skilled tradespeople, and mid-level managers typically fall into the moderate-paying job category. While the incomes in these professions may not be as high as those in the top-tier salaries, careful financial planning can still lead to significant savings and investments. For instance, a skilled tradesperson or mid-level manager may earn a steady, reliable income that allows for regular savings contributions. By adhering to a disciplined budget and prioritizing financial goals, individuals in moderate-paying jobs can accumulate savings over time and invest wisely. Moderate-paying jobs often come with the advantage of job stability and benefits, such as health insurance and retirement plans, which can further enhance financial security and support long-term wealth-building efforts.

Low-Paying Jobs: Entry-level positions, service industry jobs, and unskilled labour typically offer lower wages, making it more challenging to save and invest. Workers in these roles may struggle to cover basic living expenses, leaving little room for discretionary spending or savings. However, with careful budgeting and a commitment to financial discipline, it is still possible to set aside small amounts for savings and investments. For example, individuals in low-paying jobs might benefit from creating a strict budget, minimizing unnecessary expenses, and exploring opportunities for additional income, such as part-time work or side businesses. Additionally, investing in education and skills development can lead to higher-paying job opportunities in the future, improving the potential for savings and investment.

The higher the income, the greater the potential for savings. However, financial success is not solely determined by how much you earn but also by how much you keep and invest. Regardless of income level, adopting a disciplined approach to saving and investing can pave the way for long-term financial stability and wealth accumulation. By focusing on prudent financial management, individuals at all income levels can work towards achieving their financial goals and building a secure future.

Minimizing Expenses

Managing expenses is just as crucial as earning a substantial income when it comes to building savings. Even if you have a high-paying job, excessive spending can significantly limit your ability to save and invest. Therefore, making wise decisions about living arrangements and lifestyle choices can make a significant difference in your financial health.

Guide to Millions

Living Arrangements:

Living with Parents: If you have the option to live with your parents while starting your career, take advantage of it. Living at home can save you a significant amount of money on rent and utilities, which are often the largest expenses for young professionals. This arrangement allows you to allocate a larger portion of your income to savings and investments. Moreover, you can use this period to build an emergency fund, pay off student loans, or invest in further education or professional development.

Renting with Roommates: If living with your parents is not feasible, consider sharing a rental property with roommates. Splitting the cost of rent, utilities, and groceries can substantially reduce your living expenses. This arrangement not only lowers your monthly bills but also fosters a shared sense of financial responsibility. Additionally, living with roommates can provide a support system and make it easier to manage household tasks and expenses collectively.

Lifestyle Choices:

Clothing: Avoid the temptation to buy expensive and excessive clothing. Stick to a minimal wardrobe that meets your needs without overspending. Opt for quality over quantity, and invest in versatile pieces that can be mixed and matched. Shopping during sales, at thrift stores, or online discount retailers can also help you save money. Remember, fashion trends come and go, but financial stability is enduring.

Food: Frequently dining out can drain your finances quickly. Learn to cook and prepare your meals at home. Home-cooked meals are not only healthier but also significantly cheaper than eating out. Planning your meals, buying groceries in bulk, and utilizing leftovers can further reduce food costs. Additionally, limit spending on expensive coffee and snacks by making them at home.

Transportation: When it comes to vehicles, consider buying a reliable used car rather than a new one. New cars depreciate quickly, and a well-maintained used car can serve your needs just as well for a fraction of the cost. Furthermore, explore alternative transportation options such as public transit, biking, or walking. These options are not only cost-effective but also environmentally friendly and beneficial for your health.

Travel: Instead of expensive international travel, explore local destinations. There are often hidden gems close to home that provide enjoyable and affordable travel experiences. Consider camping, road trips, or budget-friendly travel options. By being cautious with your travel expenses, you can enjoy enriching experiences without breaking the bank. Additionally, planning trips during off-peak seasons and using travel rewards or discounts can further reduce costs.

By thoughtfully managing your expenses in these areas, you can significantly increase your ability to save and invest. Prioritizing financial discipline and making conscious spending choices will help you build a strong financial foundation, paving the way for long-term financial success and independence.

The Power of Early Savings

Starting to save early in your career can profoundly impact your financial future. This advantage is rooted in the concept of compound interest, which allows your money to grow exponentially over time. Compound interest works by earning returns on both your initial investment and the accumulated interest from previous periods. The longer your money is invested, the more it benefits from compounding, leading to substantial growth over time.

To illustrate the power of early savings, consider the example of two individuals, Alex and Jamie. Alex begins saving $500 per month at the age of 20, while Jamie starts saving the same amount at the age of 30. Both invest their savings with an average annual return of 7%.

Alex's Journey:
- Starting at age 20, Alex saves $500 per month, amounting to $6,000 annually.
- Over 40 years, Alex's total contributions amount to $240,000.
- With the power of compound interest, by age 60, Alex's investments grow to approximately $1,197,000.

Jamie's Journey:
- Starting at age 30, Jamie saves $500 per month, also amounting to $6,000 annually.
- Over 30 years, Jamie's total contributions amount to $180,000.
- By age 60, Jamie's investments grow to approximately $568,000 due to the shorter investment period.

The significant difference between Alex's and Jamie's accumulated wealth highlights the importance of starting your savings journey as early as possible. By beginning to save and invest a decade earlier, Alex benefits from an additional $629,000 compared to Jamie, even though they both contribute the same amount monthly.

This example underscores that time is a crucial factor in building wealth. The earlier you start saving, the more time your money has to grow through compounding. This means you can potentially achieve your financial goals with less effort and lower monthly contributions compared to starting later in life. Early savings provide a financial cushion, enabling you to take advantage of investment opportunities, weather economic downturns, and enjoy a comfortable retirement.

The power of early savings cannot be overstated. By prioritizing savings and investment early in your career, you set yourself up for long-term financial success and independence. The sooner you start, the more you can harness the benefits of compound interest, ensuring a secure and prosperous financial future.

Savings are the foundation of financial independence and wealth building. By understanding the relationship between your income, expenses, and occupation, you can make informed decisions that enhance your ability to save and invest. Choosing the right occupation can provide higher earning potential, but managing your expenses is equally crucial. By adopting a frugal lifestyle, living below your means, and prioritizing savings, you can build a substantial financial cushion that enables you to invest and grow your wealth.

To achieve financial independence, it's essential to start saving early in your career. The power of compound interest means that the money you save and invest today will grow exponentially over time, significantly increasing your wealth over the years. Making small sacrifices in your lifestyle choices, such as living with roommates or cooking at home, can lead to substantial savings.

Furthermore, it is important to regularly reassess and adjust your financial strategies. As your income increases, resist the temptation to inflate your lifestyle and instead, focus on increasing your savings and investments. Consistency in saving and making informed investment choices will steadily build your wealth, regardless of your income level.

Ultimately, the journey to financial independence is about making deliberate and disciplined financial choices. It's not just about how much you earn, but how much you save and invest. By taking control of your financial habits and understanding the impact of your decisions, you can set yourself on a path to financial security and prosperity. Start early, save consistently, and make smart financial decisions to achieve your financial goals and secure a prosperous future.

Chapter 2.2
THE FUNDAMENTALS OF INVESTING

When it comes to investing, having a solid foundation of knowledge is crucial. Understanding what investing entails and how it operates is the first step toward making informed decisions and growing your wealth. In this chapter, we will explore the basics of investing, different types of investments, and the expected returns from these investments.

Investing involves putting your money into various financial instruments, assets, or ventures with the expectation of generating income or profit over time. It's essential to comprehend the principles of risk and return, as all investments carry some level of risk. Generally, higher potential returns come with higher risks. Being aware of this dynamic helps in making choices that align with your financial goals and risk tolerance.

We will delve into the different types of investments, including stocks, real estate, and private businesses. Each type of investment has its own set of characteristics, benefits, and risks. Understanding these nuances is key to building a diversified investment portfolio that can weather market fluctuations.

Furthermore, this chapter will cover the concept of expected returns. Expected returns are the anticipated profits from an investment, based on historical performance and future projections. Knowing what returns to expect from different investment options helps in setting realistic financial goals and strategies.

By the end of this chapter, you will have a comprehensive understanding of the fundamentals of investing, equipping you with the knowledge needed to embark on your investment journey. This foundational knowledge is essential for making informed decisions that will help grow your wealth over time and move you closer to achieving financial independence.

Understanding Investing

Investing, at its core, is the act of allocating money with the expectation of generating a profit or return over time. This process involves putting your money into various assets or financial instruments that have the potential to increase in value, thereby growing your initial investment. The fundamental goal of investing is to achieve a positive return on your capital, which means your money works for you, rather than merely sitting idle.

One of the key principles of investing is the concept of compound interest. Compound interest refers to the process where the returns earned on an investment are reinvested, so that the returns themselves generate additional returns. For example, consider an investor who puts $100 into an investment with an annual return rate of 10%. In the first year, a 10% return on $100 would yield $10, resulting in a total of $110. In the following year, the 10% return is calculated on the new total of $110, not just the original $100. This would yield $11, making the total $121. This process continues, with each year's return being calculated on the increasingly larger amount, thus accelerating the growth of the investment.

The power of compound interest is a fundamental reason why starting to invest early can significantly impact your financial future. The longer your money is invested, the more you benefit from compounding returns, which can lead to substantial growth over time. Understanding and leveraging this concept is crucial for effective long-term investing and achieving financial goals.

Investing involves various types of assets, such as stocks, bonds, real estate, and mutual funds, each with its own risk and return profile. By carefully selecting investments and utilizing the power of compound interest, you can build wealth and work towards financial independence.

Types of Investments

Investments can be broadly categorized into two main types: property (or real estate) investments and business investments.

Property Investments: This includes purchasing residential or commercial real estate with the intention of earning rental income or capital appreciation. Property investments can offer steady income streams through rents and have the potential for significant value increases over time.

Business Investments: This category involves investing in startups, established businesses, or acquiring existing companies. Business investments can generate returns through profits, equity growth, or dividends. Investing in businesses often requires more active involvement but can yield high returns and significant control over the investment.

Both types of investments offer unique opportunities and risks, and understanding these can help you align your investment strategy with your financial goals.

Property Investments

Property investments involve acquiring real estate assets such as land, residential buildings, or commercial properties with the goal of generating financial returns. This type of investment can include a range of properties, from single-family homes and apartment complexes to office buildings, factories, and hotels.

Financial Model: The primary financial model for property investment revolves around purchasing a property and earning income through rent collected from tenants. This rental income serves as a form of passive income, meaning it requires less active management compared to other types of investments. Investors typically look for properties that offer a rental return, which is the income received from rent relative to the property's purchase price. On average, property investments yield a rental return of about 3% to 7% annually based on the property's value.

Example: Consider an investor who purchases a property valued at $100,000. If this property generates a rental return of 5% annually, the investor would earn $5,000 in rental income each year. Over time, this rental income can accumulate, providing a steady stream of passive income.

Appreciation: Besides rental income, property values have the potential to appreciate over time. This appreciation occurs when the value of the property increases due to factors such as market demand, improvements made to the property, or developments in the surrounding area. For example, if the property purchased for $100,000 appreciates in value by 2% annually, its value would increase by $2,000 in the first year. Combined with rental income, this appreciation contributes significantly to the overall return on investment.

Considerations: Investing in property also involves additional factors such as maintenance costs, property management fees, and potential vacancies, which can affect overall returns. Moreover, the real estate market can be subject to fluctuations based on economic conditions, interest rates, and regional market trends.

Overall, property investments can be a lucrative option for building wealth and generating income, especially when carefully selected and managed to optimize returns and minimize risks.

Business Investments

Business investments primarily involve buying shares or stocks of a company, which represents a stake in that business. When a company is founded, it typically decides on the number of shares it will issue, each representing a unit of ownership in the company. For instance, if a company is established with 100 shares and an initial total investment of $1,000, each share would have an initial value of $10. Investors purchase these shares, thereby owning a fraction of the company.

Growth and Returns: As the company grows and becomes more profitable, the value of each share tends to increase. This increase is driven by the company's successful operations, expansion, and overall financial health. For example, if the company's profits increase significantly, its share price may rise proportionally, reflecting the company's enhanced value and potential for future earnings. Investors benefit from this appreciation in share value, which can result in substantial financial gains.

Public Companies: Businesses that are listed on stock exchanges are known as public companies. These companies have their shares available for purchase by the general public through stock markets. Publicly traded companies must comply with regulatory requirements, including regular financial disclosures, which provides transparency to investors. This access allows investors to buy and sell shares on various stock exchanges, such as the New York Stock Exchange (NYSE) or NASDAQ, contributing to the liquidity and accessibility of stock investments.

Historical Returns: The historical average return on stock market investments is approximately 10% per year. This figure represents an average across various time periods, including years of high gains, losses, and stable performance. For example, during bull markets, investors might experience substantial gains, while in bear markets, they could face significant losses. Additionally, market volatility, economic conditions, and company performance all contribute to the variability of returns.

Considerations: Investing in stocks requires careful consideration of market trends, individual company performance, and broader economic factors. Investors should conduct thorough research, diversify their portfolios to manage risk, and stay informed about market conditions to make informed investment decisions.

Overall, business investments in stocks offer the potential for significant financial returns and ownership in successful companies. However, they also come with risks that require careful management and strategic planning.

Expected Returns on Different Investment Vehicles

Understanding the potential returns of various investment options is essential for making informed financial decisions. This section explores the typical annual returns associated with three prominent investment vehicles: bank savings accounts, property investments, and stock market investments.

Bank Savings Accounts

Bank savings accounts are one of the most secure ways to save money, offering a place to deposit funds while earning interest. The interest rates for these accounts are generally low compared to other investment options, ranging from 0% to 3% annually. For example, if you deposit $100 into a savings account with a 3% annual interest rate, you would earn $3 in interest over a year. This means that at the end of the year, your total balance would be $103. While savings accounts are low-risk and highly liquid, meaning you can access your money easily, their returns are modest and often fail to outpace inflation. Consequently, the real value of your savings can diminish over time if inflation rates exceed the interest rate earned.

Property Investments

Property investments involve purchasing real estate—whether residential, commercial, or industrial—with the aim of generating rental income and benefiting from property value appreciation. The annual returns on property investments typically range from 3% to 7%. For instance, if you acquire a property worth $100,000 and it generates a 5% annual return, you would earn $5,000 in rental income each year. In addition to rental income, property values can appreciate over time, potentially leading to significant capital gains upon selling the property. However, property investments also come with costs such as maintenance, property taxes, and management fees. Additionally, the value of real estate can be influenced by local market conditions and economic factors, which introduces some level of risk.

Stock Market Investments

Investing in the stock market is known for its potential for higher returns compared to other investment options. Historically, the stock market has averaged annual returns of around 10%. This figure represents a long-term average, including periods of substantial gains and significant losses. For example, if you invest $100 in the stock market with an average annual return of 10%, your investment would grow to $110 in the first year, $121 in the second year, and so forth, thanks to the power of compound interest. While the potential returns are attractive, stock market investments are subject to volatility. Prices of individual stocks and market indices can fluctuate significantly due to economic conditions, company performance, and market sentiment. This volatility means that while long-term returns can be robust, short-term fluctuations can lead to gains or losses.

In summary, each investment vehicle offers different risk and return profiles:

Bank Savings Accounts: Low risk and low return, with interest rates ranging from 0% to 3%. Ideal for preserving capital and maintaining liquidity.

Property Investments: Moderate risk and moderate return, with annual returns between 3% and 7%. Provides rental income and potential for capital appreciation but involves ongoing costs and management.

Stock Market Investments: Higher risk and higher return, averaging around 10% annually. Offers significant growth potential through capital gains and dividends, but with considerable volatility.

Choosing the right investment depends on your financial goals, risk tolerance, and investment horizon. Balancing these factors can help you build a diversified portfolio that aligns with your long-term financial objectives.

Comparing Returns Over Time

To illustrate the potential growth of investments over time, let's compare the returns from a bank savings account, a property investment, and a stock market investment over a 10-year period, each starting with an initial investment of $100.

Bank Savings Account (3% Annual Return)

Year	Starting Balance	Interest Earned	Ending Balance
1	$100	$3	$103
2	$103	$3.09	$106.09
3	$106.09	$3.18	$109.27
4	$109.27	$3.28	$112.55
5	$112.55	$3.38	$115.93
6	$115.93	$3.48	$119.41
7	$119.41	$3.58	$122.99
8	$122.99	$3.69	$126.68
9	$126.68	$3.80	$130.48
10	$130.48	$3.91	$134.39

Which equates of $34 earned or 34% return over 10 years

Property Investment (5% Annual Return)

Year	Starting Balance	Rent Earned	Ending Balance
1	$100	$5	$105
2	$105	$5.25	$110.25
3	$110.25	$5.51	$115.76
4	$115.76	$5.79	$121.55
5	$121.55	$6.08	$127.63
6	$127.63	$6.38	$134.01
7	$134.01	$6.70	$140.71
8	$140.71	$7.04	$147.75
9	$147.75	$7.39	$155.14
10	$155.14	$7.76	$162.90

Total earned $62 which equates to 62% over 10 years

Stock Market Investment (10% Annual Return)

Year	Starting Balance	Returns Earned	Ending Balance
1	$100	$10	$110
2	$110	$11	$121
3	$121	$12.10	$133.10
4	$133.10	$13.31	$146.41
5	$146.41	$14.64	$161.05
6	$161.05	$16.11	$177.16
7	$177.16	$17.72	$194.88
8	$194.88	$19.49	$214.37
9	$214.37	$21.44	$235.81
10	$235.81	$23.58	$259.39

Total earned $159 which equates to 159% on a $100 invested

Becoming a Millionaire Through Investing

So you now ask yourself, is that it? How can I become a millionaire by investing like this? Well, there is more to investing than just these basic principles and understanding. This is only the starting point. Reaching millionaire status through investing is an ambitious but achievable goal. While understanding basic investment principles is crucial, there's a lot more to the journey than merely grasping fundamental concepts. The path to significant wealth requires deeper insight into advanced investment strategies and a disciplined approach to managing your investments.

The Role of Leverage in Investing

One of the most impactful concepts in investing is leverage. Leverage involves using borrowed capital to increase the potential return on an investment. By borrowing money to invest, you can amplify the size of your investments, which, if managed correctly, can significantly boost your returns. For example, in property investing, using a mortgage to finance the purchase of real estate allows you to control a more valuable asset than you could with your own capital alone. This means that while you put down a small percentage of the property's value, you gain exposure to the entire asset, including its potential for appreciation and rental income.

Advanced Investment Strategies

Property Investment: Beyond understanding rental yields, successful property investors delve into market trends, property management, and value-adding strategies. Real estate investing can become highly lucrative through the strategic purchase of undervalued properties, renovations to increase property value, and leveraging market cycles for buying and selling. Knowledge of local real estate markets and economic indicators also plays a crucial role in maximizing returns.

Stock Market Investing: In the stock market, investing in individual stocks, mutual funds, or exchange-traded funds (ETFs) requires a more nuanced approach. Investors should understand different types of stocks, such as growth versus value stocks, and the importance of diversification to manage risk. Techniques such as dollar-cost averaging, which involves consistently investing a fixed amount of money regardless of market conditions, can help smooth out investment volatility and build wealth over time.

Alternative Investments: For those looking to diversify beyond traditional assets, alternative investments such as private equity, venture capital, and commodities offer additional opportunities. These investments often come with higher risk but can yield substantial returns if approached with the right strategy and due diligence.

The Importance of Knowledge and Research

Becoming a millionaire through investing also necessitates continuous education and research. The financial markets are dynamic, and staying informed about economic trends, emerging investment opportunities, and changes in regulations is crucial. Building a network of financial advisors, mentors, and peers can provide valuable insights and guidance. Additionally, understanding the impact of inflation, taxes, and fees on your investments helps in making more informed decisions and optimizing returns.

Discipline and Patience

Patience is a cornerstone of successful investing. Wealth accumulation through investing is a long-term endeavour that requires discipline to stick to your investment strategy, especially during market downturns. Market fluctuations can test your resolve, but maintaining a long-term perspective and adhering to a well-thought-out investment plan will enhance your chances of achieving millionaire status.

In summary, investing is a potent tool for wealth-building, but achieving millionaire status involves more than basic knowledge. By leveraging advanced strategies such as using borrowed capital, diversifying investments, and committing to ongoing education and disciplined practices, you can significantly enhance your financial prospects. Remember, the journey to becoming a millionaire is a marathon, not a sprint. It requires careful planning, strategic investing, and a steadfast commitment to your financial goals. Embracing these principles will set you on a path to financial success and a prosperous future.

Chapter 2.3
UNDERSTANDING BANKS

Introduction to Banking

Banks are fundamental institutions in the financial system, serving as crucial intermediaries that facilitate economic activity and contribute to overall financial stability. At their core, banks perform several vital functions that impact individuals, businesses, and the economy as a whole. Understanding these functions and how banks operate is essential for anyone interested in finance, investing, or real estate.

Core Functions of Banks

Accepting Deposits: One of the primary functions of banks is to accept deposits from individuals and businesses. These deposits can be in the form of savings accounts, checking accounts, or certificates of deposit (CDs). By accepting deposits, banks provide a safe place for individuals to store their money while earning interest. This process also contributes to the liquidity available in the financial system.

Granting Loans: Banks use the funds from deposits to provide loans to individuals and businesses. Loans can be for various purposes, including purchasing homes, starting businesses, or financing education. Banks evaluate borrowers' creditworthiness through credit checks and financial assessments to ensure they can repay the borrowed amount. Interest rates charged on loans are a key source of revenue for banks.

Offering Financial Products and Services: Banks offer a range of financial products and services beyond traditional savings and loans. These include investment services, retirement accounts, insurance products, and wealth management services. Banks also provide financial advice and planning to help clients manage their finances effectively.

The Role of Banks in the Economy

Banks play a crucial role in facilitating the flow of capital in the economy. By channelling funds from savers to borrowers, banks support economic growth and development. They help businesses expand, create jobs, and drive innovation. For individuals, banks offer access to credit, which can enable major life purchases, such as homes and cars, and support financial planning.

Understanding Banking Operations

To make informed financial decisions, it's important to understand how banks operate, particularly their lending practices. Banks assess risks, set interest rates, and determine loan terms based on various factors, including market conditions and borrower profiles. Additionally, banks are regulated by government agencies to ensure they operate soundly and protect depositors' funds.

In summary, banks are integral to the functioning of the financial system. They manage deposits, provide loans, and offer diverse financial products and services that support both personal and business financial needs. Understanding how banks operate, especially their lending practices, is essential for navigating the financial world, whether you're interested in investing, purchasing real estate, or managing personal finances.

The Basics of Banking

At its core, banking is a system designed to manage money and facilitate financial transactions. The fundamental operation of a bank revolves around accepting deposits and using those funds to provide loans. This basic model is crucial to the functioning of the financial system and plays a significant role in generating income for banks. Here's a closer examination of how banks operate and the key elements involved:

1. Deposits

Banks collect funds from customers in various forms of accounts, including savings accounts, checking accounts, and certificates of deposit (CDs). Each type of account serves different purposes and offers various features.

Savings Accounts: These accounts allow customers to deposit money while earning interest over time. They typically offer a modest interest rate and are highly liquid, meaning customers can easily access their funds.

Checking Accounts: Checking accounts are used for day-to-day transactions, such as paying bills and making purchases. While they offer less interest compared to savings accounts, they provide greater convenience and accessibility.

Certificates of Deposit (CDs): CDs are time deposits that offer higher interest rates in exchange for locking funds away for a specific period. They are less liquid than savings or checking accounts but provide a guaranteed return.

These deposits are crucial as they form the primary source of funds for banks. By pooling these deposits, banks have the resources needed to lend money to individuals and businesses.

2. Loans

Once banks receive deposits, they use a portion of these funds to grant loans to borrowers. Loans can be for various purposes, including:

Buying a Home: Mortgages allow individuals to purchase homes and repay the loan over an extended period.

Starting a Business: Business loans provide entrepreneurs with capital to start or expand their enterprises.

Funding Education: Student loans help individuals cover the cost of higher education.

The interest charged on these loans is a primary source of revenue for banks. This interest compensates the bank for the risk of lending money and for providing capital that borrowers might need for substantial investments or purchases.

3. Interest Rates

Interest rates are a critical aspect of banking operations. Banks offer interest on deposits to attract and retain customers. The rate paid on deposits is typically lower than the rate charged on loans. This difference is known as the net interest margin. It represents the bank's profit from the difference between what they earn on loans and what they pay out on deposits.

The net interest margin is a key indicator of a bank's profitability. A higher margin indicates that the bank is effectively managing its income from loans relative to the cost of deposits. Conversely, a lower margin might suggest challenges in achieving profitable lending rates or high deposit costs.

In summary, the basic operations of a bank involve accepting deposits, providing loans, and managing interest rates. Deposits provide the funds banks use to issue loans, which generate income through interest. The balance between deposit interest rates and loan interest rates, known as the net interest margin, is crucial for a bank's profitability. Understanding these fundamentals is essential for anyone interested in finance and banking, as they underpin the financial system's operation and stability.

How Banks Grant Loans

The process of granting loans involves multiple steps to ensure that banks lend responsibly while minimizing risk. Here's a detailed look at how banks typically grant loans:

1. Loan Application

The loan process begins with the borrower submitting a loan application. This application includes essential information about the borrower's financial situation, such as their income, employment status, existing debts, and the purpose of the loan. Borrowers also provide details about how they plan to use the loan funds and their proposed repayment plan. This initial application helps the bank understand the borrower's needs and basic qualifications.

2. Credit Assessment

Once the application is submitted, the bank conducts a thorough credit assessment. This involves evaluating the borrower's creditworthiness, which includes examining their credit history and credit score. The credit history reveals how the borrower has managed previous credit accounts, including any past delinquencies or defaults. Additionally, the bank reviews the borrower's income and employment status to ensure they have a stable and sufficient income to support loan repayment. Other financial indicators, such as debt-to-income ratio and savings, are also considered to assess the borrower's overall financial health and ability to repay the loan.

3. Collateral Evaluation

For secured loans, such as mortgages or auto loans, the bank requires collateral to secure the loan. Collateral is an asset that the bank can claim if the borrower fails to repay the loan. The bank performs a collateral evaluation to determine the asset's value and ensure it adequately covers the loan amount. For example, in the case of a mortgage, the bank assesses the value of the real estate being financed through an appraisal. This evaluation is crucial as it mitigates the bank's risk by providing a safeguard against potential defaults.

4. Loan Approval

Based on the results of the credit assessment and collateral evaluation, the bank makes a decision regarding the loan application. If the borrower meets the bank's criteria, the loan is approved. The bank then determines the specifics of the loan, including the amount to be lent, the interest rate, and the repayment terms. The interest rate is influenced by factors such as the borrower's creditworthiness and prevailing market rates, while the repayment terms define the duration and frequency of payments.

5. Disbursement and Repayment

Once the loan is approved and the terms are set, the bank disburses the loan funds to the borrower. This may be done as a lump sum or in installments, depending on the type of loan and its purpose. The borrower then begins making regular payments according to the agreed-upon schedule. These payments include both principal and interest. The bank monitors the borrower's payments to ensure timely repayment and may take action if payments are missed or delayed.

In summary, the loan granting process is designed to assess the borrower's ability to repay and manage risk effectively. By following these steps—application, credit assessment, collateral evaluation, approval, and disbursement—banks ensure that loans are issued responsibly and in alignment with the borrower's financial capabilities.

Why Banks Prefer Lending for Real Estate

Real estate lending is highly attractive to banks for a variety of reasons, all of which contribute to its appeal as a stable and profitable area of lending. Here's an in-depth look at why banks prefer lending for real estate:

1. Stable and Secure Collateral

Real estate is valued for its stability and tangibility. Unlike vehicles, inventory, or other types of collateral, real estate generally appreciates in value over time. This appreciation provides banks with a reliable form of collateral that can help secure their loans. If a borrower defaults on a real estate loan, the bank can seize the property and sell it to recover the outstanding amount. Because real estate tends to retain or increase in value, banks consider it a secure asset compared to other forms of collateral that may depreciate quickly or fluctuate significantly in value.

2. Low Default Rates

Historically, real estate loans, particularly residential mortgages, exhibit lower default rates compared to other types of loans. Homeowners typically prioritize their mortgage payments because losing their home is a significant consequence. The emotional and practical implications of foreclosure often drive borrowers to remain current on their mortgage payments, even during financial difficulties. This behaviour results in lower risk for banks, making real estate lending a relatively safer investment. Additionally, the structured nature of mortgage payments, including both principal and interest, helps ensure consistent revenue for banks.

3. Long-Term Revenue

Real estate loans, such as mortgages, often come with extended repayment terms ranging from 15 to 30 years. These long-term loans provide banks with a steady stream of income over a prolonged period. The extended duration allows banks to earn interest on the principal for many years, contributing to significant revenue over time. Unlike short-term loans or revolving credit, real estate loans create a predictable and sustained income flow, which enhances the bank's profitability and financial stability.

4. Government Support

Many governments actively support the real estate market through various policies and programs designed to encourage homeownership. This support can come in the form of tax incentives, loan guarantees, and subsidies, which collectively reduce the risk associated with real estate lending. For example, government-sponsored entities like Fannie Mae and Freddie Mac in the United States provide guarantees on certain types of mortgages, thereby reducing the lender's risk and increasing their willingness to offer loans. This governmental backing bolsters the stability of real estate lending and makes it a more attractive option for banks.

5. Diversification of Loan Portfolio

Including real estate loans in a bank's portfolio allows for effective diversification of risk. Diversification involves spreading investments across various asset classes to reduce exposure to any single sector or economic condition. By incorporating real estate loans, banks can balance their portfolios and mitigate the impact of downturns in other sectors. Real estate's relatively stable performance, combined with its lower default rates and long-term revenue potential, contributes to a well-rounded loan portfolio that can withstand economic fluctuations and reduce overall risk.

In conclusion, banks prefer real estate lending due to the stability and appreciation potential of real estate as collateral, the historically low default rates associated with mortgages, the long-term revenue generated from extended loan terms, the supportive role of government programs, and the benefits of portfolio diversification. These factors make real estate lending a favored choice for banks, contributing to both their financial stability and growth.

Types of Real Estate Loans

Banks offer a range of real estate loans to meet the diverse needs of borrowers. Each type of loan is designed to cater to specific purposes and comes with its own set of terms, conditions, and interest rates. Here's a closer look at the common types of real estate loans:

1. Residential Mortgages

Residential mortgages are the most common type of real estate loan and are used for purchasing or refinancing homes. These loans come in various forms, including fixed-rate and adjustable-rate mortgages (ARMs). Fixed-rate mortgages have a consistent interest rate and monthly payments throughout the life of the loan, providing stability and predictability. On the other hand, ARMs have interest rates that can change periodically based on market conditions, which might result in fluctuating monthly payments. Residential mortgages can also vary in terms, typically ranging from 15 to 30 years, impacting both monthly payments and total interest paid over the life of the loan.

2. Commercial Mortgages

Commercial mortgages are specifically designed for purchasing or refinancing commercial properties, such as office buildings, retail spaces, warehouses, and industrial facilities. These loans tend to have shorter terms, usually between 5 and 20 years, compared to residential mortgages. Additionally, commercial mortgages often come with higher interest rates and more stringent qualification requirements. This is due to the higher risk associated with commercial properties and the potential for greater market fluctuations affecting business operations.

3. Home Equity Loans and Lines of Credit

Home equity loans and lines of credit (HELOCs) allow homeowners to borrow against the equity they have built in their properties. Home equity loans provide a lump sum of money with a fixed interest rate and repayment term. In contrast, HELOCs offer a revolving line of credit with a variable interest rate, allowing homeowners to borrow as needed up to a certain limit. These loans are often used for home improvements, debt consolidation, or significant expenses like education costs.

4. Construction Loans

Construction loans are short-term loans used to finance the construction of new properties. These loans typically cover the costs of building materials, labor, and other construction expenses. They are disbursed in stages, known as "draws," based on the progress of the construction. Once the construction is completed, the construction loan is usually converted into a long-term mortgage, known as a "permanent mortgage," which is used to pay off the construction loan and finance the property for the long term.

5. Investment Property Loans

Investment property loans are designed for purchasing properties intended for rental income or resale. These loans are tailored for investors looking to acquire properties for generating income through rent or capital gains from future sales. Investment property loans typically come with higher interest rates and stricter lending criteria compared to residential mortgages due to the increased risk associated with rental properties and potential market volatility.

In summary, understanding the different types of real estate loans helps borrowers choose the right financing option for their specific needs, whether they are buying a home, investing in commercial properties, or funding construction projects. Each loan type has distinct features and requirements, making it crucial to evaluate them based on individual financial situations and goals.

The Role of Banks in the Real Estate Market

Banks play a crucial role in the real estate market, influencing various aspects from property purchases to broader economic trends. Their lending activities are central to facilitating real estate transactions and shaping market dynamics. Here's a closer look at how banks impact the real estate market:

1. Enabling Homeownership

One of the primary functions of banks in the real estate market is to provide mortgages, which are essential for enabling homeownership. By offering loans to individuals and families, banks make it possible for more people to purchase homes who might otherwise be unable to afford them. This access to homeownership supports social stability and enhances economic mobility by allowing individuals to invest in property and build equity over time. Homeownership also fosters community ties and stability, contributing to a more settled and engaged population.

2. Stimulating Economic Activity

Real estate transactions have a ripple effect on the economy. When a property is bought or sold, it stimulates a range of related activities, including construction, renovation, and real estate services. Banks, by providing the necessary financing, facilitate these transactions and thus contribute to economic growth. The demand for construction services, home improvement products, and real estate professionals creates jobs and drives economic activity in these sectors. Additionally, real estate transactions generate tax revenues for local governments, further supporting community development and public services.

3. Market Stability

Banks play a critical role in maintaining stability within the real estate market. Through responsible lending practices, banks assess borrowers' creditworthiness and evaluate the value of the collateral, such as property, before issuing loans. By ensuring that borrowers have the capacity to repay their loans and that properties provide adequate security, banks help mitigate the risk of defaults and foreclosures. This careful vetting process helps to stabilize the market, preventing extreme fluctuations in property values and maintaining confidence among buyers and sellers.

4. Influencing Price Trends

Banks' lending policies significantly influence real estate price trends. Interest rates, loan-to-value ratios, and other lending criteria can affect property demand and, consequently, prices. For instance, when banks offer lower interest rates, borrowing becomes cheaper, increasing the affordability of mortgages. This can lead to higher demand for properties, driving up prices. Conversely, stringent lending requirements and higher interest rates can reduce the pool of qualified buyers, tempering price growth and potentially leading to price stabilization or declines.

Banks are pivotal in shaping the real estate market through their lending activities. By enabling homeownership, stimulating economic activity, maintaining market stability, and influencing price trends, banks play an essential role in the overall health and dynamics of the real estate sector. Understanding these functions helps illustrate the interconnectedness of financial institutions and real estate markets, highlighting the importance of responsible lending practices and economic policies.

Banks play a critical role in the economy by providing essential financial services, including real estate lending. Their preference for lending in the real estate sector is driven by the stability and security of property as collateral, lower default rates, long-term revenue potential, and government support. By understanding how banks operate and their role in real estate lending, individuals and businesses can make informed decisions when seeking financing for property investments. However, it is also important to recognize the challenges and risks associated with real estate lending and to approach it with a strategic and informed mindset.

The Role of Banks in Business Operations

Banks are essential to the economy, serving as intermediaries between capital providers and businesses that require funding to grow and sustain their operations.

Their involvement is critical to the smooth functioning of the economic system, as they offer various types of loans and credit facilities that enable businesses to purchase assets, acquire equipment, finance day-to-day operations, and manage cash flow. The financing provided by banks not only supports business growth but also helps maintain stability and improve operational efficiency. Understanding how banks finance businesses, the types of loans available, and the criteria for lending is crucial for anyone involved in business management or aspiring to start a business. This chapter explores the different ways banks provide financing, the types of loans offered, and how they assess the financial health of businesses, highlighting the indispensable role banks play in supporting and sustaining business operations.

1. Asset Financing

Businesses often require significant capital expenditures to purchase or upgrade assets such as real estate, machinery, and equipment. Banks offer specialized loans for asset financing, allowing businesses to acquire these critical assets without depleting their working capital. Two primary forms of asset financing include equipment loans and real estate loans.

Equipment Loans: These loans are used specifically to purchase machinery or equipment essential for business operations. The equipment itself typically serves as collateral, reducing the risk for the lender. For example, a manufacturing company might take out an equipment loan to buy new production machinery. The terms of these loans vary based on the asset's lifespan and value, typically ranging from three to seven years. Equipment loans provide businesses with the financial flexibility to invest in necessary tools and technology, thereby enhancing productivity and efficiency without upfront capital strain

Real Estate Loans: When businesses need to acquire commercial property or expand their premises, real estate loans provide the necessary funds. These loans often have longer terms, ranging from 15 to 30 years, reflecting the extended useful life of the property. Like equipment loans, real estate loans are generally secured by the property itself, offering banks a stable form of collateral.

By spreading the cost of property acquisition over time, real estate loans enable businesses to expand their physical presence, meet operational needs, and pursue growth opportunities.

2. Vehicle Financing

For businesses that require vehicles for their operations—such as delivery trucks, company cars, or service vans—vehicle financing is a critical aspect of their financial strategy. Banks offer vehicle loans specifically designed for the purchase of these assets.

Vehicle Loans: These loans are similar to equipment loans but are tailored for the purchase of vehicles. The vehicle serves as collateral for the loan, which mitigates the lender's risk. Repayment terms for vehicle loans typically range from three to five years, depending on the vehicle's expected useful life. Vehicle loans provide businesses with the ability to maintain or expand their fleet without incurring significant upfront costs, ensuring that transportation needs are met efficiently.

3. Credit Lines for Business Operations

Managing cash flow is a fundamental aspect of running a successful business. Banks offer credit lines that help businesses cover short-term expenses, manage cash flow fluctuations, and invest in new opportunities.

Business Lines of Credit: A business line of credit provides a revolving credit facility that businesses can draw upon as needed. Unlike traditional loans, where the borrower receives a lump sum and begins repaying immediately, a line of credit offers greater flexibility. Interest is only paid on the amount drawn, not the total credit limit. This flexibility allows businesses to manage cash flow effectively, cover unexpected expenses, and seize opportunities without taking on large amounts of debt. For example, a retailer might use a line of credit to purchase additional inventory ahead of a busy shopping season, ensuring they can meet demand without straining their cash reserves.

Trade Credit: While not directly offered by banks, trade credit is another form of short-term financing that plays a crucial role in business operations. Suppliers extend trade credit to businesses, allowing them to purchase goods and services on credit, typically with payment terms of 30 to 90 days. Businesses often use trade credit in conjunction with bank credit lines to manage their operational needs efficiently. Trade credit provides the flexibility to manage cash flow and maintain smooth operations, even during periods of financial strain.

4. Supporting Growth and Expansion

Banks are integral to financing various aspects of business operations, particularly when it comes to growth and expansion. Whether businesses are looking to open new locations, increase inventory, or scale operations, banks offer financing solutions tailored to support these objectives.

Long-Term Loans: For businesses pursuing significant growth, long-term loans provide the capital needed for large-scale investments. These loans, which may include SBA (Small Business Administration) loans, are typically repaid over several years, allowing businesses to spread the cost of expansion over time. Long-term loans are often used for substantial projects, such as constructing new facilities, acquiring another business, or launching a major product line.

SBA Loans: The U.S. Small Business Administration (SBA) partners with banks to offer loans that help small businesses grow and expand. These loans are partially guaranteed by the SBA, reducing the risk for lenders and making it easier for small businesses to obtain financing. SBA loans are commonly used for purchasing real estate, equipment, or inventory, and for refinancing existing debt to improve cash flow.

Equipment Financing: As mentioned earlier, equipment financing is a vital tool for businesses looking to expand their operations by acquiring new machinery or technology. By enabling businesses to invest in state-of-the-art equipment, banks help them improve efficiency, increase production capacity, and maintain a competitive edge in the market.

In conclusion, banks play a pivotal role in business operations by providing the financial tools necessary for growth, stability, and efficiency. Through asset financing, vehicle loans, credit lines, and support for expansion, banks enable businesses to navigate the challenges of the marketplace, manage their finances effectively, and pursue their strategic goals. Understanding the various financing options available and how banks assess business health is crucial for any business owner or manager aiming to achieve long-term success.

How Banks Assess Loan Applications

Banks carefully assess the financial health and capacity of businesses before granting loans. This assessment process helps ensure that loans are issued responsibly and that borrowers have the ability to repay. Key factors considered in the loan evaluation process include:

1. Creditworthiness

Banks examine the credit history and credit score of the business and its owners to evaluate creditworthiness. A strong credit history indicates a history of responsible borrowing and repayment, making the business a lower-risk borrower. A high credit score can improve the likelihood of loan approval and favourable terms.

2. Financial Statements

Banks review financial statements, including balance sheets, income statements, and cash flow statements, to assess the business's financial health. These documents provide insights into profitability, liquidity, and overall financial stability. Strong financial statements demonstrate the business's ability to generate income and manage expenses effectively.

3. Business Plan

A well-developed business plan outlines the business's goals, strategies, and financial projections. Banks use this information to evaluate the viability of the business and its ability to repay the loan. A comprehensive business plan demonstrates the business's preparedness and strategic approach to achieving its objectives.

4. Collateral

For secured loans, banks assess the value of the collateral offered by the borrower. Collateral serves as security for the loan and provides the bank with a tangible asset that can be claimed in the event of default. The value and condition of the collateral are crucial factors in determining the loan amount and terms.

5. Cash Flow

Banks analyse cash flow statements to determine the business's ability to generate sufficient cash to cover loan payments. Positive cash flow indicates that the business can meet its financial obligations and manage day-to-day operations effectively.

Understanding how banks finance businesses, the types of loans available, and the criteria for lending is essential for business owners and aspiring entrepreneurs. Banks play a pivotal role in supporting business operations, from funding asset purchases and managing cash flow to facilitating growth and expansion. By offering various types of loans and credit facilities, banks provide the necessary financial resources for businesses to thrive and succeed.

Effective loan management and responsible borrowing are critical for maintaining financial stability and achieving long-term success. By leveraging the financial support offered by banks and adhering to sound financial practices, businesses can navigate challenges, seize opportunities, and build a prosperous future.

Chapter 2.4
THE POWER OF LEVERAGE

Introduction to Leverage

Leverage is a powerful financial tool that allows investors to amplify their returns by using borrowed money to increase their investment capacity. In the context of property investment, leverage enables investors to purchase real estate with a combination of their own funds and borrowed capital, typically through a mortgage. By leveraging their investments, investors can control larger assets and potentially generate higher returns compared to investing solely with their own money.

How Leverage Works in General

Leverage involves using borrowed funds to finance an investment. The idea is to invest a portion of your own money (equity) and borrow the rest, thereby increasing the total amount available for investment. The returns generated from the investment are then distributed across both the borrowed and the invested funds, effectively magnifying the potential gains (or losses).
Here's a simple illustration:
- **Equity**: The investor's own money used for the investment.
- **Debt**: The borrowed funds used to finance the investment.
- **Total Investment**: The sum of equity and debt.

If an investment increases in value, the gain is calculated on the total investment, while the cost of debt (interest) is fixed. This results in a higher return on the equity portion. Conversely, if the investment decreases in value, the loss is also magnified.

Leverage in Property Investment

In property investment, leverage is commonly used through mortgages. Investors can buy properties by putting down a small percentage of the property's value as a down payment and borrowing the rest from a bank or other lender. The leverage ratio is the proportion of borrowed funds to the total property value.

Example of Leverage in Property Investment

Let's consider an example where an investor uses leverage to purchase a property with a 5% rental return on the property value. The investor puts down 20% of the property's value as a down payment and borrows the remaining 80%.

1. **Property Value**: $100,000
2. **Down Payment (Equity)**: 20% of $100,000 = $20,000
3. **Loan Amount (Debt)**: 80% of $100,000 = $80,000
4. **Rental Return**: 5% of $100,000 = $5,000 annually

Without leverage, if the investor bought the property outright with $100,000, the annual rental return would be 5% on the entire amount, or $5,000.

Calculating Returns with Leverage

When leverage is used, the return on equity (ROE) changes significantly. Here's how:

1. **Annual Rental Income**: $5,000
2. **Loan Principal Repayment**: Assuming no interest for simplicity, the borrowed $80,000 does not affect the net rental income calculation.

The net rental income is simply the annual rental income:

- **Net Rental Income**: $5,000

To calculate the return on equity (ROE):

- **Return on Equity (ROE)**: Net Rental Income / Equity
- **ROE**: $5,000 / $20,000 = 25%

In this example, the investor's equity of $20,000 generates a 25% return due to leverage, compared to a 5% return if the property was purchased outright. This demonstrates the power of leverage in amplifying returns.

Advantages of Using Leverage in Property Investment

1. **Increased Purchasing Power**: Leverage allows investors to buy more expensive properties or multiple properties with the same amount of initial capital.
2. **Higher Returns on Equity**: As demonstrated in the example, leverage can significantly boost the return on the investor's equity.
3. **Diversification**: By using leverage, investors can spread their capital across multiple properties, reducing risk through diversification.
4. **Tax Benefits**: In many jurisdictions, the interest paid on a mortgage loan can be tax-deductible, reducing the overall cost of borrowing.

Risks of Using Leverage in Property Investment

While leverage can amplify returns, it also increases risk. It's essential to understand and manage these risks:

1. **Increased Risk of Losses**: If property values decline, the losses are magnified due to the high level of debt. The investor is still obligated to repay the loan regardless of the property's performance.

2. **Cash Flow Challenges**: The need to make regular interest payments can strain cash flow, especially if the property is not generating sufficient rental income or if there are unexpected expenses.
3. **Market Fluctuations**: Real estate markets can be volatile. Economic downturns, changes in interest rates, or shifts in demand can impact property values and rental income.
4. **Foreclosure Risk**: If the investor fails to make loan payments, the lender can foreclose on the property, potentially resulting in the loss of the investment.

Mitigating Risks of Leverage

To mitigate the risks associated with leverage, investors should:
1. **Conduct Thorough Due Diligence**: Carefully research the property, market conditions, and potential rental income before making an investment.
2. **Maintain Adequate Cash Reserves**: Keep a financial cushion to cover loan payments, property maintenance, and unexpected expenses.
3. **Monitor Market Conditions**: Stay informed about economic trends, interest rates, and real estate market conditions to make timely decisions.
4. **Use Conservative Leverage Ratios**: Avoid over-leveraging by keeping debt levels manageable and within a comfortable risk tolerance.

Leverage is a powerful tool in property investment that allows investors to amplify their returns by using borrowed funds. By understanding how leverage works and carefully managing the associated risks, investors can significantly enhance their investment performance. In the example provided, using leverage increased the return on equity from 5% to 25%, demonstrating the potential benefits of this strategy.

However, it's crucial to approach leverage with caution, conducting thorough research and maintaining financial discipline. When used wisely, leverage can be a game-changer in property investment, enabling investors to achieve their financial goals and build substantial wealth over time.

10-Year Example of Returns on a $100,000 Property with $20,000 Equity Invested and 5% Rental Income

Here's a table illustrating the returns over 10 years for a $100,000 property with $20,000 equity invested and a 5% rental income on the property value each year. This example assumes no interest rate for simplicity and no compounding return on equity.

Year	Property Value	Rental Income (5% of Property Value)	Equity	Annual Rental Income	Total Equity at Year End
1	$100,000	$5,000	$20,000	$5,000	$25,000
2	$100,000	$5,000	$20,000	$5,000	$30,000
3	$100,000	$5,000	$20,000	$5,000	$35,000
4	$100,000	$5,000	$20,000	$5,000	$40,000
5	$100,000	$5,000	$20,000	$5,000	$45,000
6	$100,000	$5,000	$20,000	$5,000	$50,000
7	$100,000	$5,000	$20,000	$5,000	$55,000
8	$100,000	$5,000	$20,000	$5,000	$60,000
9	$100,000	$5,000	$20,000	$5,000	$65,000
10	$100,000	$5,000	$20,000	$5,000	$70,000

Explanation
1. **Property Value**: Remains constant at $100,000 throughout the 10 years for simplicity.

2. **Rental Income**: Calculated as 5% of the property value ($100,000), which equals $5,000 annually.
3. **Equity**: The initial equity is $20,000.
4. **Annual Rental Income**: The rental income earned each year, which is $5,000.
5. **Total Equity at Year End**: The sum of the initial equity and the annual rental income accumulated over the years.

In this example, the total equity grows by $5,000 each year from the rental income. After 10 years, the total equity amounts to $70,000, starting from an initial equity investment of $20,000. This straightforward approach demonstrates the consistent return on investment generated by rental income without factoring in compounded returns or interest rates.

Now in this example the return on "Invested" money of $20.000 is $5.000 which equates to **25% return per year**, and all together throughout the 10 years is $50.000 which is **250% of return**

Which is significantly bigger than getting **5% returns per year and 50% returns in 10 years** if we didn't use leverage

Once equity is build up in a property throughout a few years, one can use that equity for a loan for another property, and then the income is multiplied.

Which means when you build up equity value in first property in amount of 20% of new property, you can use this equity at the bank to give you a loan for another property.

Chapter 2.5
PROPERTY INVESTING BASICS

Introduction to Property Investments

Property investments involve purchasing real estate such as land, residential buildings (houses, apartment complexes), or commercial properties (office buildings, factories, storage units, hotels). The primary financial model for property investment is to buy property and then collect rent from tenants. This rent is a form of passive income, and on average, property investments yield a rental return of 3% to 7% annually on the property's total value.

For instance, if an investor buys a property worth $100,000 and rents it out with a 5% annual return, they would earn $5,000 in rent each year. Additionally, property values can appreciate over time, contributing to the overall return on investment.

Basic Principles of Property Investment

1. Location: The location of the property significantly impacts its value and rental income. Properties in prime locations with good infrastructure, schools, and amenities typically attract higher rents and appreciate more in value.

2. Research and Due Diligence: Thorough research on market conditions, property values, and potential rental income is essential before making any investment. Understanding the local real estate market trends can help investors make informed decisions.

3. Property Condition and Management: Well-maintained properties attract better tenants and yield higher rents. Proper property management, including regular maintenance and addressing tenant concerns promptly, ensures a steady rental income and preserves property value.

4. Financing Options: Understanding different financing options and their implications on cash flow and returns is crucial. Mortgages, loans, and other financing methods should be carefully considered to optimize the investment.

5. Risk Management: Diversifying investments across different properties and locations can mitigate risks. Additionally, maintaining adequate insurance and having a financial cushion for unexpected expenses are essential for long-term stability.

Maximizing Returns by Paying More Than the Minimum Loan Amount

When investing in property, many individuals opt for a 30-year mortgage to purchase their homes or investment properties. While this standard approach is manageable for most, it often results in a substantial amount of interest paid over the life of the loan. By doubling up on minimum payments, investors can significantly reduce the interest paid, build equity faster, and ultimately position themselves to acquire additional properties sooner. This chapter explores the benefits and financial impacts of accelerating mortgage payments, using a practical example to illustrate the differences between the two models.

Understanding Standard Loan Repayment
The Traditional 30-Year Mortgage
A standard 30-year mortgage spreads the loan repayments over three decades, making monthly payments relatively low and affordable. However, this extended term means that the interest paid over the life of the loan can be nearly as much as the principal borrowed.

Example Scenario:
- Property Value: $300,000
- Down Payment: 20% ($60,000)
- Loan Amount: $240,000
- Interest Rate: 4%

Guide to Millions

- Loan Term: 30 years
- Monthly Payment: $1,146.81 (principal and interest)

Total Interest Paid Over 30 Years

Using the above parameters, let's calculate the total interest paid over the life of the loan.
- Total Payments: 360 (30 years × 12 months)
- Total Amount Paid: $1,146.81 × 360 = $412,851.60
- Total Interest Paid: $412,851.60 - $240,000 = $172,851.60

Accelerated Loan Repayment

Doubling Up Payments

If the borrower doubles the minimum payment amount, they not only pay off the loan faster but also save a significant amount on interest. Doubling up the payment accelerates the principal reduction, which in turn reduces the amount of interest accrued.

Example Scenario:
- Monthly Payment: $2,293.62 (double the standard payment)
- New Loan Term: Calculated based on accelerated payments

Calculating the New Loan Term and Total Interest Paid

To determine the new loan term and total interest, we need to adjust the amortization schedule.

New Loan Term

With doubled payments, the loan term is reduced dramatically. Using a mortgage calculator, we find that the loan term is reduced to approximately 10 years.
- Total Payments: 120 (10 years × 12 months)
- Total Amount Paid: $2,293.62 × 120 = $275,234.40
- Total Interest Paid: $275,234.40 - $240,000 = $35,234.40

Comparing the Two Models

Financial Impact

1. Standard 30-Year Mortgage**:
   - Monthly Payment: $1,146.81
   - Total Interest Paid: $172,851.60
   - Loan Term: 30 years
2. Accelerated Payment Plan:
   - Monthly Payment: $2,293.62
   - Total Interest Paid: $35,234.40
   - Loan Term: 10 years

Savings and Equity Growth

By doubling up payments, the borrower saves $137,617.20 in interest over the life of the loan. Additionally, they build equity much faster, owning the property outright in just 10 years instead of 30.

Potential for Additional Investments

The faster repayment not only saves money on interest but also frees up significant cash flow much sooner. This increased equity and freed-up capital can be reinvested into new properties, accelerating the growth of passive income and building wealth.

Avoiding the Dream Home Trap

Common Pitfall: The Dream Home

Many people fall into the trap of buying their dream home, maxing out their loan capability with maximum weekly payments they can afford. While this approach provides a luxurious living situation, it often results in prolonged debt and minimal flexibility for future investments.

Strategic Approach: Buy What You Can Afford

Instead of purchasing the most expensive home possible, investors should focus on buying a property they can afford to repay much sooner. Here's why:

1. Lower Purchase Price: A more affordable property means lower monthly payments and less interest paid over time.

2. Faster Equity Growth: Paying off the loan faster increases equity more rapidly, providing financial security and opportunities for reinvestment.

3. Financial Flexibility: Reduced debt burden allows for more flexibility in managing finances, investing in additional properties, and weathering economic downturns.

Example of Strategic Buying

Consider an investor choosing between a $300,000 home and a $200,000 home. Both scenarios assume a 20% down payment and a 4% interest rate.

1. $300,000 Home:
   - Down Payment: $60,000
   - Loan Amount: $240,000
   - Monthly Payment: $1,146.81
   - Total Interest Paid Over 30 Years: $172,851.60

2. $200,000 Home:
   - Down Payment: $40,000
   - Loan Amount: $160,000
   - Monthly Payment: $764.54
   - Total Interest Paid Over 30 Years: $114,150.40

If the investor doubles payments for the $200,000 home:
- Monthly Payment: $1,529.08
- New Loan Term: Approximately 10 years

- Total Interest Paid: $23,386.72

Benefits of the Strategic Approach

By choosing the $200,000 home and doubling payments, the investor pays significantly less in interest ($23,386.72 vs. $172,851.60) and builds equity faster. In 10 years, they can own the property outright and reinvest the savings into additional properties.

Conclusion

Paying more than the minimum loan amount can have a profound impact on property investment returns. Doubling up payments on a 30-year mortgage reduces the loan term to about 10 years, saving a significant amount in interest and accelerating equity growth. This approach provides financial flexibility and opportunities for further investments, ultimately leading to faster wealth accumulation.

Investors should avoid the common pitfall of purchasing their dream home at the maximum loan capacity. Instead, they should focus on buying affordable properties they can repay quickly, maximizing their financial potential and paving the way for future investments. By adopting a strategic approach to property investment and leveraging accelerated loan payments, investors can build substantial wealth and achieve their financial goals much sooner.

Understanding Capital Appreciation in Property Investment

Introduction to Capital Appreciation

Capital appreciation refers to the increase in the value of an asset over time. In the context of property investment, it signifies the rise in the market value of real estate properties. This appreciation is a critical factor for investors, as it contributes significantly to the overall return on investment (ROI). In this chapter, we will explore the average and high rates of property value increases, the factors influencing these increases, and how to identify potential investment properties with high appreciation potential. We will also provide a detailed example of ROI over 20 years, considering rental returns, rent increases, and property value appreciation.

Average and High Rates of Property Value Increase

Average Increase in Property Value

Historically, real estate has been a stable investment with a steady rate of appreciation. On average, property values in the United States have increased by about 3% to 5% annually. This rate can vary significantly depending on the location, economic conditions, and market demand.

High Increase in Property Value

In some cases, properties can experience higher rates of appreciation, ranging from 6% to 10% or more annually. These high rates are typically observed in rapidly growing urban areas, locations undergoing significant economic development, or regions experiencing high demand for housing due to factors like population growth or desirable amenities.

Factors Influencing High Property Value Appreciation

Several factors can influence the appreciation rate of a property. Understanding these factors can help investors identify properties with high appreciation potential.

Location

Location is one of the most critical determinants of property value appreciation. Properties in prime locations, such as city centres, near public transportation, in good school districts, or close to major employment hubs, tend to appreciate faster.

Economic Growth

Regions experiencing robust economic growth often see higher property value appreciation. Job creation, business expansion, and infrastructure development contribute to increased demand for housing, driving up property values.

Supply and Demand

The balance of supply and demand in the real estate market significantly impacts property values. In areas with limited housing supply and high demand, property values tend to rise more rapidly.

Development and Amenities

Proximity to amenities such as shopping centres, parks, schools, and healthcare facilities can boost property values. Additionally, properties in areas with ongoing or planned development projects often experience higher appreciation rates.

Demographic Trends

Demographic shifts, such as an influx of young professionals or retirees to a particular area, can influence property values. Areas that attract specific demographic groups often see increased demand and, consequently, higher property values.

Government Policies

Government policies, including tax incentives, zoning regulations, and infrastructure investments, can impact property values. Favourable policies that promote development and investment in specific areas can lead to higher appreciation rates.

Example: Return on Investment Over 20 Years

Guide to Millions

To illustrate the impact of capital appreciation and rental returns on ROI, let's consider a property investment example over 20 years.

Investment Details
- Initial Property Value: $500,000
- Down Payment: 20% ($100,000)
- Loan Amount: $400,000
- Interest Rate: 4%
- Loan Term: 30 years
- Annual Rental Return: 5% of property value
- Annual Rent Increase: 3%
- Annual Property Value Appreciation: 3% to 5%

Yearly Breakdown

Let's calculate the ROI considering two scenarios: a 3% and a 5% annual property value appreciation rate.

Scenario 1: 3% Annual Property Value Appreciation
1. Initial Year:
   - Property Value: $500,000
   - Annual Rental Income: $500,000 × 5% = $25,000
2. Year 1:
   - Property Value: $500,000 × (1 + 3%) = $515,000
   - Annual Rental Income: $25,000 × (1 + 3%) = $25,750
3. Year 2:
   - Property Value: $515,000 × (1 + 3%) = $530,450
   - Annual Rental Income: $25,750 × (1 + 3%) = $26,522.50

This pattern continues, with both the property value and rental income increasing annually.

Scenario 2: 5% Annual Property Value Appreciation

1. Initial Year:
   - Property Value: $500,000
   - Annual Rental Income: $25,000
2. Year 1:
   - Property Value: $500,000 × (1 + 5%) = $525,000
   - Annual Rental Income: $25,000 × (1 + 3%) = $25,750
3. Year 2:
   - Property Value: $525,000 × (1 + 5%) = $551,250
   - Annual Rental Income: $25,750 × (1 + 3%) = $26,522.50

This pattern also continues, with both the property value and rental income increasing annually.

Total Return on Investment

Scenario 1: 3% Annual Property Value Appreciation
- Property Value After 20 Years:
  - $500,000 × (1 + 3%)^20 = $500,000 × 1.806 = $903,000
- Total Rental Income Over 20 Years:
  - The sum of increasing annual rental income over 20 years.
  - Calculated using the formula for the sum of a geometric series.

Scenario 2: 5% Annual Property Value Appreciation
- Property Value After 20 Years:
  - $500,000 × (1 + 5%)^20 = $500,000 × 2.653 = $1,326,500
- Total Rental Income Over 20 Years:
  - The sum of increasing annual rental income over 20 years.
  - Calculated using the formula for the sum of a geometric series.

Detailed Calculation

Using the geometric series formula for total rental income and the final property value:

1. Scenario 1 (3% appreciation):
   - Property Value After 20 Years: $903,000
   - Total Rental Income: Approximately $644,646 (using the sum of a geometric series formula)
2. Scenario 2 (5% appreciation):
   - Property Value After 20 Years: $1,326,500
   - Total Rental Income: Approximately $734,660 (using the sum of a geometric series formula)

ROI Calculation

1. Scenario 1:
   - Total Investment Value After 20 Years: $903,000 (property value) + $644,646 (rental income) = $1,547,646
   - Initial Investment: $100,000 (down payment)
   - ROI: ($1,547,646 - $100,000) / $100,000 × 100% = 1447.65%
2. Scenario 2:
   - Total Investment Value After 20 Years: $1,326,500 (property value) + $734,660 (rental income) = $2,061,160
   - Initial Investment: $100,000 (down payment)
   - ROI: ($2,061,160 - $100,000) / $100,000 × 100% = 1961.16%

Conclusion

Capital appreciation plays a crucial role in property investment, significantly impacting overall ROI. By understanding the factors that influence property value appreciation and selecting properties in prime locations with strong growth potential, investors can maximize their returns. As illustrated in the example, even moderate appreciation rates combined with rental income can lead to substantial ROI over the long term.

When looking for investment properties, consider factors such as location, economic growth, supply and demand, development, demographics, and government policies. By strategically selecting properties with high appreciation potential and managing rental income effectively, investors can achieve significant wealth accumulation and financial success in the real estate market.

The Impact of Minimum Deposit on Property Investment Returns

When buying a property, the amount of the down payment can significantly influence the return on investment (ROI). For first-time home buyers, there are often various incentives and benefits to ease the financial burden, such as reduced down payment requirements and exemptions from certain taxes. In Australia, first-time home buyers can purchase property with only a 10% down payment and are exempt from stamp duty, which is typically around 5% of the property value. This chapter will explore the effects of making the minimum down payment on property investment returns, comparing scenarios with 10% and 20% down payments. Additionally, we will discuss the implications for further property investments and how to strategically utilize the smallest possible down payment to maximize ROI.

Benefits for First-Time Home Buyers in Australia
Lower Down Payment Requirement

First-time home buyers in Australia can benefit from a reduced down payment requirement, allowing them to purchase a property with just 10% of the property's value. This lower initial outlay makes property ownership more accessible and enables buyers to enter the market sooner.

Stamp Duty Exemption

    First-time home buyers are also exempt from paying stamp duty, a tax on property transactions that typically amounts to 5% of the property's value. This exemption can result in substantial savings and improve overall investment returns.

ROI Example with Different Down Payment Scenarios

    Let's compare the ROI of a property investment with 10% and 20% down payments, using the example of a $500,000 property from the previous chapter.

Investment Details
- Property Value: $500,000
- Annual Rental Return: 5% of property value
- Annual Rent Increase: 3%
- Annual Property Value Appreciation: 3% to 5%
- Loan Term: 30 years
- Interest Rate: 4%

Scenario 1: 10% Down Payment
1. Initial Investment:
   - Down Payment: 10% of $500,000 = $50,000
   - Loan Amount: $450,000
2. Annual Rental Income:
   - Year 1: 5% of $500,000 = $25,000
   - Year 2: $25,000 × (1 + 3%) = $25,750
   - Continues to increase by 3% annually.
3. Property Value Appreciation:
   - Year 1: $500,000 × (1 + 3%) = $515,000
   - Year 2: $515,000 × (1 + 3%) = $530,450

- Continues to increase by 3% annually.
4. Loan Repayment:
   - Monthly Payment: $450,000 loan at 4% interest over 30 years ≈ $2,148
   - Annual Payment: $2,148 × 12 = $25,776
5. Net Rental Income:
   - Year 1: $25,000 (rental income) - $25,776 (loan repayment) = -$776
   - In subsequent years, net income improves as rental income increases.

Scenario 2: 20% Down Payment

1. Initial Investment:
   - Down Payment: 20% of $500,000 = $100,000
   - Loan Amount: $400,000
2. Annual Rental Income:
   - Year 1: 5% of $500,000 = $25,000
   - Year 2: $25,000 × (1 + 3%) = $25,750
   - Continues to increase by 3% annually.
3. Property Value Appreciation:
   - Year 1: $500,000 × (1 + 3%) = $515,000
   - Year 2: $515,000 × (1 + 3%) = $530,450
   - Continues to increase by 3% annually.
4. Loan Repayment:
   - Monthly Payment: $400,000 loan at 4% interest over 30 years ≈ $1,910
   - Annual Payment: $1,910 × 12 = $22,920
5. Net Rental Income:
   - Year 1: $25,000 (rental income) - $22,920 (loan repayment) = $2,080
   - In subsequent years, net income increases as rental income rises.

Total ROI Comparison

Scenario 1: 10% Down Payment

Guide to Millions

- Property Value After 20 Years (assuming 3% annual appreciation):
  - $500,000 × (1 + 3%)^20 ≈ $903,000
- Total Rental Income Over 20 Years:
  - Sum of annual rental income increasing by 3% annually ≈ $644,646
- Total Investment Value:
  - Property Value + Total Rental Income ≈ $903,000 + $644,646 = $1,547,646
- Initial Investment:
  - $50,000 (down payment)
- **ROI:**
  - ($1,547,646 - $50,000) / $50,000 × 100% ≈ **2995.29%**

Scenario 2: 20% Down Payment

- Property Value After 20 Years (assuming 3% annual appreciation):
  - $500,000 × (1 + 3%)^20 ≈ $903,000
- Total Rental Income Over 20 Years:
  - Sum of annual rental income increasing by 3% annually ≈ $644,646
- Total Investment Value:
  - Property Value + Total Rental Income ≈ $903,000 + $644,646 = $1,547,646
- Initial Investment:
  - $100,000 (down payment)
- **ROI:**
  - ($1,547,646 - $100,000) / $100,000 × 100% ≈ **1447.65%**

Analysis

From the comparison above, it's clear that a lower down payment (10%) significantly boosts the ROI compared to a higher down payment (20%). This is due to the higher leverage effect, where the investor's initial capital generates greater returns relative to the investment size. However, it's essential to consider the increased risk and higher monthly mortgage payments associated with a lower down payment.

Implications for Further Property Investments

After the first property purchase, subsequent investments typically require a higher down payment, often around 20%. To maximize ROI, investors should seek opportunities to make the smallest possible down payment while ensuring the investment remains financially viable. Strategies to achieve this include:

1. Leveraging Equity

As the value of the first property increases, investors can leverage the built-up equity to finance additional property purchases. This approach allows for lower down payments on new investments and maximizes the investor's capital efficiency.

2. Utilizing Investment Loans

Some lenders offer specialized investment loans with lower down payment requirements. Investors should research and compare loan options to find the most favourable terms that align with their investment strategy.

3. Joint Ventures

Partnering with other investors can reduce the required down payment for each party. Joint ventures allow investors to pool resources and acquire properties that might be otherwise unaffordable individually.

4. Government Programs and Incentives

Certain government programs and incentives can provide financial assistance or lower down payment requirements for property investments. Staying informed about available programs can help investors take advantage of these opportunities.

Conclusion

Paying the minimum deposit when purchasing a property can significantly enhance ROI by leveraging borrowed funds to generate higher returns on the initial investment. For first-time home buyers in Australia, benefits such as reduced down payment requirements and stamp duty exemptions further amplify these returns. When planning further property investments, investors should explore strategies to minimize down payments, such as leveraging equity, utilizing investment loans, forming joint ventures, and taking advantage of government programs.

By strategically managing down payments and leveraging financial incentives, investors can optimize their property investment returns, build wealth more rapidly, and achieve their financial goals more effectively.

The Power of Equity Building in Multiple Property Investments

Investing in multiple properties can significantly amplify your returns and build wealth over time. The strategy involves leveraging the equity built in existing properties to finance the purchase of additional properties. This chapter provides a detailed example of how an investor can grow their portfolio by buying new properties when the equity in their existing properties builds up to 20% of the value of a new property. We'll use a basis of $500,000 for each new property, and demonstrate the value increases, rental income increases, total equity, and total ROI over a 20-year period.

Investment Assumptions

Before we delve into the calculations, let's outline the assumptions:
1. Initial Property Value: $500,000
2. Initial Down Payment: 20% of $500,000 = $100,000

3. Annual Property Value Appreciation: 4%
4. Annual Rental Return: 5% of property value
5. Annual Rent Increase: 3%
6. Loan Term: 30 years
7. Interest Rate: 4%

Year-by-Year Calculation

Year 1
1. Property Value: $500,000
2. Equity: $100,000 (down payment)
3. Loan Amount: $400,000
4. Annual Rental Income: $500,000 × 5% = $25,000
5. Total Equity: $100,000 (initial equity)

Year 2
1. Property Value: $500,000 × (1 + 4%) = $520,000
2. Equity: $120,000 (previous equity + appreciation)
3. Annual Rental Income: $25,000 × (1 + 3%) = $25,750
4. Total Equity: $120,000

Year 3
1. Property Value: $520,000 × (1 + 4%) = $540,800
2. Equity: $140,800 (previous equity + appreciation)
3. Annual Rental Income: $25,750 × (1 + 3%) = $26,523
4. Total Equity: $140,800

Year 4
1. Property Value: $540,800 × (1 + 4%) = $562,432
2. Equity: $162,432 (previous equity + appreciation)
3. Annual Rental Income: $26,523 × (1 + 3%) = $27,319

4. Total Equity: $162,432

Year 5
1. Property Value: $562,432 × (1 + 4%) = $584,929
2. Equity: $184,929 (previous equity + appreciation)
3. Annual Rental Income: $27,319 × (1 + 3%) = $28,139
4. Total Equity: $184,929

At this point, the equity in the first property exceeds $100,000, which is 20% of the value of a new $500,000 property. Therefore, the investor can now purchase a second property.

Purchase of Second Property (Year 6)

Second Property Details:
1. Property Value: $500,000
2. Down Payment: $100,000 (from the equity of the first property)
3. Loan Amount: $400,000
4. Annual Rental Income: $500,000 × 5% = $25,000

First Property Details:
1. Remaining Equity: $84,929 (after down payment for the second property)
2. Annual Rental Income: $28,139 × (1 + 3%) = $29,083

Combined Total Equity and Income (Year 6)

1. Total Property Value: $584,929 (first property) + $500,000 (second property) = $1,084,929
2. Total Equity: $84,929 (first property) + $100,000 (second property) = $184,929
3. Total Annual Rental Income: $29,083 (first property) + $25,000 (second property) = $54,083

Subsequent Years

The process continues with the properties appreciating in value and generating rental income. When the combined equity of all properties reaches 20% of the value of a new property, another property is purchased.

Let's outline the major milestones:

Year 10
1. Property Values:
   - First Property: $584,929 × (1 + 4%)^5 ≈ $711,375
   - Second Property: $500,000 × (1 + 4%)^5 ≈ $608,326
2. Total Equity: Combining equity from both properties, the equity exceeds $200,000, allowing for the purchase of a third property.

Third Property Details:
1. Property Value: $500,000
2. Down Payment: $100,000 (from the equity of the first and second properties)
3. Loan Amount: $400,000
4. Annual Rental Income: $500,000 × 5% = $25,000

Year 15
By Year 15, the investor now has three properties, each continuing to appreciate and generate rental income.
1. Combined Property Values: The properties continue to appreciate, and the investor is ready to purchase a fourth property.
2. Annual Rental Income: All properties contribute to a growing rental income stream.

Year 20
At Year 20, the investor's portfolio has grown significantly.

Guide to Millions

1. Combined Property Values:
   - First Property: $500,000 × (1 + 4%)^20 ≈ $1,095,383
   - Second Property: $500,000 × (1 + 4%)^15 ≈ $900,945
   - Third Property: $500,000 × (1 + 4%)^10 ≈ $740,122
   - Fourth Property: $500,000 × (1 + 4%)^5 ≈ $608,326
   - Fifth Property: $500,000 (newly purchased)

2. Total Equity: The equity across all properties has grown, allowing for further property purchases and wealth accumulation.

3. Annual Rental Income: The total rental income from all properties contributes to a significant passive income stream.

Summary of ROI Over 20 Years

Let's summarize the overall ROI over 20 years, including property value appreciation, rental income, and equity growth.

Initial Investment:
- First Property Down Payment: $100,000

Final Portfolio Value:
- Combined Property Values ≈ $4,344,776

Total Equity:
- Equity across all properties ≈ $1,344,776 (after accounting for down payments and loan amounts)

Total Rental Income:
- Cumulative rental income over 20 years ≈ $1,200,000

ROI Calculation:
- Total Value + Total Equity + Total Rental Income - Initial Investment
- ($4,344,776 + $1,344,776 + $1,200,000 - $100,000) / $100,000 × 100% ≈ 6,789.55%

Conclusion

By strategically leveraging the equity built in existing properties to purchase new properties, investors can significantly amplify their returns and build a substantial property portfolio over time. The example provided demonstrates the power of equity building and compound growth through property value appreciation and rental income increases. Over a 20-year period, starting with an initial $100,000 investment can lead to a portfolio worth millions, generating substantial passive income and equity. This approach highlights the importance of strategic property investment and the benefits of leveraging equity to maximize ROI.

Chapter 2.6
BUSINESS INVESTMENT BASICS

The Vital Role of Businesses in the Economy

Businesses are the backbone of the economy, driving innovation, creating jobs, and generating wealth. They operate in various forms and sizes, from small mom-and-pop shops to large multinational corporations. This chapter explores the essential role businesses play in economic development, job creation, and societal progress. It will also examine different types of businesses and provide a comprehensive list of industries based on economic sectors: primary, secondary, and tertiary.

The Importance of Businesses in the Economy

Job Creation
      One of the most critical contributions of businesses to the economy is job creation. Businesses, regardless of their size, provide employment opportunities for millions of people, which in turn helps to reduce poverty and improve living standards. Employment not only offers individuals a source of income but also contributes to their personal development and social integration.
      Small businesses, in particular, are significant job creators. They often provide employment opportunities in local communities, offering a variety of roles that contribute to the social fabric of the area. On the other hand, large corporations can create thousands of jobs and often provide extensive benefits and opportunities for career advancement.

Innovation and Economic Growth
      Businesses drive innovation by developing new products, services, and technologies that improve quality of life and boost economic growth. Through

research and development, companies create solutions that meet consumer needs, enhance productivity, and open up new markets. Innovation also fosters competition, which can lead to better products and services at lower prices for consumers.

The economic growth spurred by businesses is evident in increased GDP, higher standards of living, and improved infrastructure. Successful businesses generate profits, which can be reinvested in further growth, creating a virtuous cycle of development and prosperity.

Wealth Generation and Distribution

Businesses contribute to wealth generation by producing goods and services that have value in the marketplace. The profits earned by businesses can be distributed in several ways: reinvested in the business for growth, paid out as dividends to shareholders, or used to pay salaries and wages to employees. This distribution of wealth helps to stimulate the economy, as employees and shareholders spend their earnings, creating demand for goods and services and supporting other businesses.

Community and Social Development

Beyond their economic contributions, businesses play a crucial role in community and social development. Many businesses engage in corporate social responsibility (CSR) initiatives, supporting local communities through charitable donations, volunteer efforts, and sustainable practices. These activities can have a positive impact on education, healthcare, and the environment, contributing to the overall well-being of society.

Types of Businesses

Businesses can be categorized based on their size, ownership structure, and whether they are listed on a stock exchange. Understanding these distinctions is essential for grasping the diversity and complexity of the business world.

Small and Medium-Sized Enterprises (SMEs)

Small and medium-sized enterprises (SMEs) are businesses with a limited number of employees and relatively low revenue compared to larger corporations. SMEs are typically more flexible and adaptive, allowing them to respond quickly to market changes and innovate efficiently. They play a crucial role in job creation and economic growth, particularly in local communities.

Large Corporations

Large corporations are companies with substantial revenues and a significant number of employees. These businesses often operate on a global scale, with extensive resources and influence. Large corporations can drive significant economic growth through substantial investments in research and development, infrastructure, and employee training.

Listed Companies

Listed companies are businesses whose shares are traded on stock exchanges. These companies have access to capital markets, allowing them to raise funds by issuing shares to the public. Being listed often means adhering to strict regulatory requirements and providing transparency through regular financial disclosures.

Private Companies

Private companies are owned by a small group of investors or a single entity and do not trade their shares publicly. These businesses have more flexibility in their operations and decision-making processes, as they are not subject to the same level of scrutiny and regulatory requirements as listed companies.

Economic Sectors and Industries

Businesses operate across a wide range of industries, which can be categorized into three primary economic sectors: primary, secondary, and tertiary. Each sector encompasses various industries that contribute to the overall functioning of the economy.

<u>Primary Sector</u>

The primary sector involves the extraction and harvesting of natural resources. It includes industries that focus on agriculture, mining, forestry, and fishing. These industries provide raw materials that are essential for the functioning of other economic sectors.

<u>1. Agriculture</u>: Farms, organic food producers, dairy farms, poultry farms, vineyards, fruit orchards, vegetable growers, flower nurseries, and rice paddies.
<u>2. Mining</u>: Coal mining companies, gold mining firms, copper mines, iron ore mining companies, diamond mining corporations, bauxite mining companies, silver mining firms, lithium mining companies, zinc mines, and rare earth element mining companies.
<u>3. Forestry</u>: Logging companies, timber production firms, paper pulp mills, sawmills, wood pellet manufacturers, forest management companies, reforestation firms, tree nurseries, wood processing companies, and biomass energy producers.
<u>4. Fishing</u>: Commercial fishing fleets, aquaculture farms, seafood processing companies, fish hatcheries, shellfish farming businesses, shrimp farming

companies, tuna fishing firms, salmon farming businesses, seaweed harvesting companies, and recreational fishing charters.

Secondary Sector

The secondary sector involves the processing and manufacturing of goods. It includes industries that transform raw materials into finished products, contributing significantly to industrial development and economic growth.

1. Manufacturing: Automobile manufacturers, electronics companies, textile mills, furniture factories, chemical production companies, pharmaceutical manufacturers, aerospace companies, food and beverage processors, toy manufacturers, and metal fabrication companies.

2. Construction: Residential construction firms, commercial building companies, infrastructure development companies, road construction firms, bridge building companies, home renovation contractors, civil engineering firms, skyscraper construction companies, industrial construction firms, and demolition companies.

3. Energy Production: Power plants, renewable energy companies, oil and gas companies, coal power plants, wind farm developers, solar panel manufacturers, nuclear energy companies, hydroelectric power producers, geothermal energy companies, and biomass energy producers.

4. Textile and Apparel: Clothing manufacturers, textile mills, fashion design houses, sportswear companies, workwear manufacturers, fabric production companies, home textile manufacturers, apparel accessories producers, footwear manufacturers, and children's clothing companies.

Tertiary Sector

The tertiary sector involves the provision of services rather than goods. This sector encompasses a broad range of industries that offer services to consumers and businesses, playing a critical role in modern economies.

1. Retail: Supermarkets, department stores, online retailers, specialty boutiques, convenience stores, electronics retailers, furniture stores, clothing retailers, toy stores, and bookshops.
2. Finance and Insurance: Banks, insurance companies, investment firms, credit unions, mortgage brokers, stockbrokers, financial advisory firms, pension funds, venture capital firms, and mutual funds.
3. Healthcare: Hospitals, private clinics, dental practices, pharmacies, nursing homes, medical laboratories, rehabilitation centers, mental health services, health insurance companies, and telemedicine providers.
4. Education: Schools, universities, online education platforms, tutoring services, vocational training centres, language schools, educational publishers, private academies, e-learning companies, after-school programs, and education consultancy firms.
5. Hospitality and Tourism: Hotels, resorts, travel agencies, tour operators, restaurants, cruise lines, event planning companies, theme parks, holiday rental services, and car rental companies.
6. Transportation and Logistics: Airlines, shipping companies, trucking firms, rail transport companies, public transit providers, logistics and warehousing companies, freight forwarders, courier services, moving companies, and ride-sharing services.
7. Information Technology: Software development companies, IT consulting firms, internet service providers, cybersecurity companies, cloud service providers, hardware manufacturers, telecommunications companies, data analytics firms, tech support services, and digital marketing agencies.
8. Media and Entertainment: Television networks, film production companies, publishing houses, music production companies, video game developers, streaming services, advertising agencies, event management companies, radio stations, and talent management agencies.
9. Professional Services: Law firms, accounting firms, consulting companies, engineering firms, architectural firms, marketing agencies, human resources companies, real estate agencies, graphic design studios, and public relations firms.

10. Utilities: Water supply companies, electricity providers, natural gas companies, waste management firms, recycling companies, telecommunications providers, internet service providers, public utility companies, energy distributors, and utility maintenance companies.

Businesses are the lifeblood of the economy, driving job creation, innovation, and economic growth. They operate in various forms and sizes, contributing to wealth generation and societal progress. By understanding the types of businesses and the industries they operate in, we gain a deeper appreciation for their role in shaping our world.

The economic sectors—primary, secondary, and tertiary—encompass a wide range of industries that collectively form the backbone of the global economy. Each sector plays a vital role in ensuring the availability of goods and services, supporting economic stability, and fostering growth. From the extraction of natural resources to the provision of advanced services, businesses are integral to the functioning of our economy and society.

Investing in Listed Equities

Investing in listed equities, or publicly traded stocks, is a fundamental way for individuals to build wealth over the long term. This chapter explores the basics of investing in listed equities, the historical returns of the stock market, the nature of market movements, and the distinction between trading and investing. Through simple examples and explanations, we will understand why investing in equities is a long-term endeavour and why even the smartest investors cannot consistently predict market movements to achieve extraordinary returns.

How Investing in Listed Equities Works

Listed equities are shares of companies that are publicly traded on stock exchanges like the New York Stock Exchange (NYSE), NASDAQ, or the London

Stock Exchange (LSE). When you buy a share of stock, you are essentially buying a small ownership stake in that company. As a shareholder, you have the potential to benefit from the company's growth and profitability through capital appreciation (an increase in the stock price) and dividends (a portion of the company's profits distributed to shareholders).

Basic Steps to Invest in Equities

1. Open a Brokerage Account: To invest in equities, you need to open a brokerage account with a firm that facilitates stock trading.
2. Research and Select Stocks: Conduct research to identify companies you believe will perform well over time. Consider factors like the company's financial health, industry position, and growth prospects.
3. Buy Shares: Use your brokerage account to purchase shares of the selected companies.
4. Monitor and Hold: Keep track of your investments and hold them for the long term, allowing time for the companies to grow and generate returns.

Historical Returns of the Stock Market

The stock market has historically provided substantial returns to long-term investors. Over the past century, the average annual return of the U.S. stock market, represented by the S&P 500 index, has been around 10% before inflation. This return includes both capital appreciation and dividends.

Example of Long-Term Growth

Consider an investor who invested $10,000 in the S&P 500 index in 1980. By 2020, assuming an average annual return of 10%, that investment would have grown to approximately $358,000. This example illustrates the power of compounding returns over a long period.

Understanding Market Movements

The stock market does not move in a straight line. Instead, it experiences fluctuations due to various factors, including economic conditions, corporate performance, investor sentiment, and geopolitical events. Market movements can be categorized into three main types:

1. Upward Movement (Bull Market)

A bull market is characterized by rising stock prices. Investors are generally optimistic, and economic conditions are favourable. Bull markets can last for several years and provide substantial returns to investors.

2. Downward Movement (Bear Market)

A bear market occurs when stock prices decline significantly, typically by 20% or more from recent highs. Bear markets are often driven by economic recessions, corporate earnings declines, or negative investor sentiment. While bear markets can be challenging, they are also temporary phases in the broader market cycle.

3. Sideways Movement

In a sideways market, stock prices remain relatively stable, fluctuating within a narrow range. During these periods, investors may not see significant gains or losses. Sideways markets can occur when there is uncertainty or a lack of strong economic drivers.

The Unpredictability of Market Movements

One of the fundamental truths about investing in equities is that market movements are inherently unpredictable. Even the most experienced and knowledgeable investors cannot consistently predict short-term market fluctuations. If they could, they would achieve extraordinary returns far exceeding the average market growth. However, most investors, including professionals, achieve returns close to the average market performance over the long term.

Why Predictions Are Difficult

1. Complex Factors: Market movements are influenced by a myriad of factors, including economic data, corporate earnings, geopolitical events, and investor behaviour. The interplay of these factors makes accurate predictions challenging.
2. Behavioural Biases: Investors are subject to behavioural biases such as overconfidence, herd behaviour, and emotional decision-making, which can lead to irrational market movements.
3. Randomness: Markets often exhibit random price movements, making it difficult to distinguish between meaningful trends and noise.

Trading vs. Investing

It is essential to distinguish between trading and investing. Trading involves buying and selling stocks frequently to profit from short-term price movements. This approach requires constant monitoring of the market, a high tolerance for risk, and often results in high transaction costs.

Investing for the Long Term

Investing, on the other hand, is a long-term strategy that involves buying and holding stocks for several years, if not decades. The goal of investing is to benefit from the long-term growth of companies and the overall economy. Long-term investors focus on the fundamentals of the companies they invest in and are less concerned with short-term market fluctuations.

Benefits of Long-Term Investing

1. Compounding Returns: By reinvesting dividends and holding stocks over a long period, investors can benefit from the compounding effect, where returns generate additional returns.

2. Reduced Risk: Long-term investing reduces the impact of short-term volatility. Historically, the longer the holding period, the lower the likelihood of losing money in the stock market.

3. Tax Efficiency: Long-term investments are often subject to lower capital gains tax rates compared to short-term trades.

Example of Long-Term Investing

Let's consider an investor who buys $10,000 worth of shares in a diversified portfolio of stocks. Over the next 20 years, the portfolio grows at an average annual rate of 8%, a conservative estimate compared to the historical average. By the end of the 20-year period, the investment would have grown to approximately $46,610.

Market Volatility Over Time

During these 20 years, the investor would experience various market conditions, including bull markets, bear markets, and sideways movements. Despite these fluctuations, the long-term growth trend would result in substantial wealth accumulation.

Investing in listed equities is a powerful way to build wealth over the long term. While market movements can be unpredictable and short-term volatility can be daunting, the historical performance of the stock market demonstrates the potential for significant returns. By focusing on long-term investing rather than short-term trading, investors can benefit from compounding returns, reduced risk, and tax efficiency. Understanding the nature of market movements and maintaining a disciplined, long-term approach is key to achieving financial success through equity investments.

Investing in Private Businesses

Investing in private businesses can be a highly rewarding venture, offering significant opportunities for growth, innovation, and financial returns. Unlike public companies, private businesses are not listed on stock exchanges and typically have fewer regulatory requirements and greater operational flexibility. This chapter delves into the mechanics of investing in private companies, exploring profit multiples, mergers and acquisitions (M&A), and the pros and cons of private equity investing.

Understanding Private Companies and Profit Multiples

Private companies are owned by a small number of investors or a single entity and do not trade their shares publicly. This ownership structure allows for greater control and flexibility but can also pose challenges in terms of liquidity and valuation. One common method for valuing private companies is using a profit multiple, which is a key metric in determining the purchase price of a business.

Profit Multiples Explained

A profit multiple is a valuation metric that compares a company's price to its annual profits. The multiple represents the number of times the annual profit is included in the purchase price. For instance, a profit multiple of 5 means the purchase price is five times the company's annual profit.

Example:
- Annual Profit: $1,000,000
- Profit Multiple: 5
- Purchase Price: $1,000,000 x 5 = $5,000,000

Guide to Millions

This method is straightforward and widely used because it provides a quick estimate of a company's value based on its profitability. However, the actual multiple can vary depending on factors such as the industry, growth potential, risk profile, and market conditions.

Factors Influencing Profit Multiples

1. Industry: Different industries have varying average profit multiples. For instance, technology companies might have higher multiples due to their growth potential, while manufacturing businesses might have lower multiples due to slower growth and higher capital requirements.
2. Growth Potential: Companies with strong growth prospects typically command higher multiples as investors are willing to pay a premium for future profitability.
3. Risk Profile: Businesses with stable and predictable earnings usually have higher multiples compared to those with volatile or uncertain profits.
4. Market Conditions: Economic conditions and market trends can influence profit multiples. In a bullish market, multiples tend to be higher due to increased investor confidence and demand for assets.

Mergers and Acquisitions (M&A) in Private Businesses

Mergers and acquisitions are common strategies for growth, diversification, and gaining competitive advantages in the business world. M&A activities can involve large private corporations as well as small private businesses, each with its unique set of considerations and processes.

M&A for Large Private Corporations

For large private corporations, M&A can be a complex and lengthy process involving significant due diligence, negotiation, and regulatory approvals. These transactions often require the expertise of investment banks, legal advisors, and financial consultants.

Key Steps in M&A for Large Corporations:

1. Strategic Planning: The acquiring company identifies potential targets that align with its strategic objectives, such as expanding market share, entering new markets, or acquiring new technologies.

2. Due Diligence: A thorough evaluation of the target company's financial health, operations, legal status, and market position is conducted to assess the potential risks and benefits of the acquisition.

3. Valuation: The target company's value is determined using various methods, including profit multiples, discounted cash flow (DCF) analysis, and comparable company analysis.

4. Negotiation: Terms of the acquisition, including the purchase price, payment structure, and post-acquisition plans, are negotiated between the parties.

5. Regulatory Approval: Depending on the jurisdiction and industry, the acquisition may require approval from regulatory bodies to ensure compliance with antitrust laws and other regulations.

6. Integration: Post-acquisition, the two companies undergo an integration process to align their operations, cultures, and systems, aiming to realize synergies and achieve the strategic goals of the acquisition.

M&A for Small Private Businesses

For small private businesses, M&A transactions tend to be simpler and quicker, though they still require careful planning and execution. Small business acquisitions often involve individual investors, private equity firms, or other small businesses looking to expand.

Key Steps in M&A for Small Businesses:

1. Target Identification: The acquiring party identifies small businesses that match their acquisition criteria, such as geographical location, industry, and size.

2. Preliminary Evaluation: Initial discussions and evaluations are conducted to determine the viability of the acquisition. This includes reviewing financial statements, business operations, and market position.

3. Due Diligence: A detailed examination of the target business's financial health, legal status, and operational efficiency is carried out to identify potential risks and opportunities.

4. Valuation and Offer: The target business is valued, typically using profit multiples or other relevant methods, and an offer is made to the owners.

5. Negotiation: Terms of the acquisition are negotiated, including the purchase price, payment terms, and transition plans.

6. Closing and Transition: The transaction is finalized, and ownership is transferred. The transition process involves integrating the acquired business into the existing operations of the acquiring party.

Private Equity Investing: Pros and Cons

Private equity investing involves investing capital into private companies, often with the aim of improving their performance and eventually selling them at a profit. Private equity firms typically raise funds from institutional investors and high-net-worth individuals to acquire and manage a portfolio of private companies.

Pros of Private Equity Investing

1. High Potential Returns: Private equity investments can offer substantial returns, especially if the firms successfully improve the performance and value of the portfolio companies.

2. Active Management: Private equity firms often take an active role in managing and improving the operations of the companies they invest in, leading to better performance and higher returns.

3. Diversification: Private equity provides diversification opportunities beyond traditional public market investments, potentially reducing overall portfolio risk.

4. Access to Growth Companies: Private equity investors often have access to high-growth companies that are not available in public markets, allowing them to capitalize on emerging opportunities.

5. Long-Term Focus: Private equity investments typically have a longer investment horizon, allowing for strategic planning and operational improvements that may not be possible with short-term public market pressures.

Cons of Private Equity Investing

1. Illiquidity: Private equity investments are generally illiquid, meaning investors cannot easily sell their stakes and may have to wait several years to realize returns.

2. High Risk: Investing in private companies can be risky due to factors such as market volatility, operational challenges, and regulatory changes. The potential for high returns comes with the risk of significant losses.

3. High Fees: Private equity firms often charge substantial management and performance fees, which can eat into the overall returns for investors.

4. Complexity: Private equity transactions can be complex and require significant due diligence, legal expertise, and financial analysis.

5. Limited Transparency: Private companies are not required to disclose the same level of information as public companies, making it harder for investors to assess the true financial health and performance of the business.

Investing in private businesses offers unique opportunities for substantial returns, innovation, and economic impact. Understanding the valuation methods, such as profit multiples, and the processes involved in M&A for both large and small businesses is crucial for successful investments. Private equity investing comes with its set of advantages and challenges, requiring careful consideration and strategic planning..

Ultimately, investing in private businesses requires a thorough understanding of market dynamics, financial metrics, and strategic planning. By navigating these complexities, investors can unlock significant value and contribute to the growth and development of private enterprises.

Investing in Small Private Businesses

Investing in small private businesses can be a highly lucrative venture, offering opportunities for substantial returns and direct involvement in business growth. Unlike investing in listed equities, which often comes with higher multiples and limited leverage options, private business investments allow for more tailored and strategic financial maneuvers. This chapter explores the intricacies of investing in small private businesses, focusing on valuation multiples, leverage, passive investments, and a comparative analysis with listed equities.

Valuation Multiples in Small Private Businesses

One of the most critical aspects of investing in small private businesses is determining the company's value. Valuation multiples are a commonly used method for this purpose. A multiple is a factor applied to a company's earnings, revenue, or another financial metric to estimate its value.

Earnings Multiples

Earnings multiples are among the most common valuation methods for small private businesses. The multiple is applied to the company's annual earnings (EBITDA - Earnings Before Interest, Taxes, Depreciation, and Amortization) to determine its value.

Example Calculation:
- Annual EBITDA: $500,000
- Earnings Multiple: 4
- Business Value: $500,000 x 4 = $2,000,000

Revenue Multiples

For businesses with unstable or minimal earnings but strong revenue, revenue multiples can be more appropriate. The multiple is applied to the company's annual revenue to estimate its value.

Example Calculation:
- Annual Revenue: $1,000,000
- Revenue Multiple: 1.5
- Business Value: $1,000,000 x 1.5 = $1,500,000

Factors Influencing Multiples

1. Industry: Multiples vary widely across industries. High-growth sectors like technology often command higher multiples than more stable sectors like manufacturing.
2. Growth Potential: Businesses with significant growth prospects attract higher multiples.
3. Risk Profile: Companies with stable, predictable earnings generally have higher multiples than those with volatile earnings.
4. Market Conditions: Economic conditions and investor sentiment can influence multiples. In a booming economy, multiples tend to be higher.

Leverage in Private Business Investments

Leverage is a powerful financial tool that involves using borrowed capital to finance the purchase of a business. This strategy can significantly amplify returns, making it a popular method among investors. However, it also introduces additional risk, as the obligation to repay the borrowed funds remains regardless of the business's performance. Leveraged buyouts (LBOs) are a common approach to acquiring small private businesses, allowing investors to gain control over larger assets with a smaller initial capital outlay.

Leveraged Buyouts (LBOs)

In a leveraged buyout, the investor uses a mix of equity (their own money) and debt (borrowed money) to purchase a business. The acquired business's future cash flows are then utilized to service the debt. This strategy is advantageous because it enables investors to maximize their potential returns while minimizing the amount of their own capital at risk. The key to a successful LBO is ensuring that the business generates enough cash flow to comfortably cover the debt repayments.

Example Calculation:
Let's consider an example with a business valued at four times its annual profit.
- Annual Profit: $500,000
- Purchase Price (4x Profit): $2,000,000
- Investor Equity (25% of Purchase Price): $500,000
- Debt Financing (75% of Purchase Price): $1,500,000

In this scenario, the investor contributes $500,000 of their own money and borrows $1,500,000 to finance the purchase. The business's annual profit of $500,000 will be used to cover the debt service costs.

Debt Service Calculation:
Assuming the borrowed funds come with an interest rate of 5% per annum, and the debt is structured to be repaid over a period of 10 years, the annual debt service (which includes both principal and interest payments) can be calculated as follows:
- Annual Interest: $1,500,000 x 5% = $75,000
- Annual Principal Repayment: $1,500,000 / 10 years = $150,000
- Total Annual Debt Service: $75,000 + $150,000 = $225,000

Net Cash Flow to Investor:

After servicing the debt, the remaining cash flow is the profit available to the investor:

- Annual Profit: $500,000
- Total Annual Debt Service: $225,000
- Net Cash Flow to Investor: $500,000 - $225,000 = $275,000

In this example, the investor's initial equity contribution of $500,000 generates an annual cash flow of $275,000 after debt servicing. This represents a substantial return on the investor's capital.

Benefits of Leverage

1. Enhanced Returns: Using debt can significantly boost returns on the investor's equity. In the example above, the investor's initial $500,000 results in an annual return of $275,000, representing a 55% return on equity.
2. Tax Advantages: Interest payments on borrowed funds are typically tax-deductible, which can reduce the overall tax liability and enhance the investment's profitability.
3. Control Over Larger Assets: Leverage allows investors to acquire and control larger businesses than they could afford using only their own capital.

Risks of Leverage

1. Increased Financial Risk: High levels of debt can increase the financial risk of the investment. If the business's cash flows decline, meeting debt obligations can become challenging.
2. Interest Rate Risk: Fluctuations in interest rates can impact the cost of debt, potentially increasing the burden on the business.
3. Bankruptcy Risk: Failure to service the debt can lead to bankruptcy, resulting in the loss of the invested capital and potential legal consequences.

Conclusion

Leverage is a powerful strategy for investors looking to maximize their returns in private business investments. By utilizing a combination of equity and debt, investors can control larger assets and enhance their potential profits. However, it is essential to carefully consider the risks associated with leverage and ensure that the business generates sufficient cash flow to cover debt obligations comfortably. Successful leveraged buyouts require thorough due diligence, strategic planning, and effective management to navigate the complexities and risks involved.

Passive Investment Strategy

Business with Management in Place

To avoid buying oneself a job, it's crucial to invest in businesses with competent management in place. The goal of a passive investment strategy is to earn returns without becoming entangled in the day-to-day operations of the business. This means identifying businesses where the current management team is not only capable but also experienced and dedicated. A strong management team can ensure that the business continues to run smoothly and efficiently, even in the absence of active oversight from the investor. This allows the investor to focus on strategic decisions and other investment opportunities rather than becoming bogged down in operational details. In essence, the investor relies on the expertise and leadership of the existing management to maintain and grow the business, ensuring a hands-off yet profitable investment.

Ensuring Profitability

Ensuring the profitability of a business is another cornerstone of a successful passive investment strategy. The ideal business should have a robust track record of consistent profitability, demonstrating its ability to generate stable income over time. This involves looking for businesses with healthy financial statements, steady revenue streams, and sustainable profit margins. Such businesses are less likely to face sudden downturns and more likely to continue delivering returns to investors.

A profitable business not only provides immediate returns through dividends or profit sharing but also increases in value over time, enhancing the investor's equity. When acquiring such a business through leverage, the investor can use the business's ongoing profits to service the debt, thereby amplifying returns on the initial investment. This makes the leveraged buyout more attractive and financially viable.

Additionally, consistent profitability is a sign of operational efficiency and market competitiveness. It indicates that the business has a solid customer base, effective cost management, and a product or service that meets market demands. For the passive investor, this means a lower risk of financial instability and a higher likelihood of long-term success. Thus, by investing in a business with competent management and a proven track record of profitability, the investor can achieve a truly passive investment that yields substantial returns without requiring constant oversight or intervention.

Comparing Private Business Investments with Listed Equities

Investing in small private businesses and listed equities presents two distinct approaches, each with its own set of advantages and challenges. Understanding the differences in valuation, leverage, control, liquidity, and risk is crucial for making informed investment decisions.

Valuation Multiples

One of the key differences between private businesses and listed equities is the valuation multiples. Listed equities typically trade at higher multiples due to greater liquidity, transparency, and broader investor demand.

Public Company EBITDA Multiple: 10
Private Company EBITDA Multiple: 4
Differences in Using Leverage

Listed Equities

In the stock market, most individual investors do not use leverage when investing in listed equities. This means that investors use their own capital to buy shares, and the return on investment is directly tied to the performance of the stock without borrowing. This minimizes risk but also limits potential returns since the investment growth depends solely on the equity's performance.

Private Businesses

Investing in private businesses often involves using significant leverage, especially in leveraged buyouts (LBOs). Investors use a mix of debt and equity to acquire a business, relying heavily on borrowed capital. This strategy can significantly enhance returns because the debt allows investors to control larger assets with less capital. However, it also increases financial risk, as failure to generate sufficient cash flow can lead to insolvency.

Control and Influence

Investors in private businesses usually have more control and influence over operations and strategic decisions compared to investors in public companies.

Private Business: Direct involvement, board seats, strategic input.
Public Company: Limited influence, especially for small shareholders.

Liquidity

Liquidity is another critical difference between the two investment types.

Listed Equities: Traded daily on exchanges, offering greater liquidity and ease of buying and selling shares.

Private Businesses: Less liquid, often requiring a longer time horizon to find a buyer and complete transactions.

Risk and Return

Private business investments can offer higher returns due to lower multiples and effective use of leverage, but they also come with higher risk.

Private Businesses: Potential for significant returns, higher risk.

Listed Equities: Generally more stable, lower risk, and lower potential returns.

Case Study: Investing in a Small Manufacturing Business

Business Overview
Industry: Manufacturing
Annual Revenue: $2,000,000
Annual EBITDA: $400,000
Asking Price: $1,600,000 (4x EBITDA)

Investment Plan
Purchase Price: $1,600,000
Investor Equity: $400,000
Debt Financing: $1,200,000

Debt Terms
Interest Rate: 6%
Loan Term: 5 years

Annual Debt Service Calculation
Annual Interest: $1,200,000 x 6% = $72,000

Annual Principal Repayment: $1,200,000 / 5 = $240,000
Total Annual Debt Service: $312,000

Net Cash Flow to Investor
Annual EBITDA: $400,000
Debt Service: $312,000
Net Cash Flow: $88,000

Return on Equity
Investor Equity: $400,000
Annual EBITDA: $400,000
Return on Equity: 100%

Passive Investment Strategy
The investor retains the existing management team, providing them with equity incentives to ensure alignment of interests. The business continues to operate efficiently, generating steady cash flows to service the debt and provide returns to the investor.

Comparative Analysis with Listed Equities

Listed Equities Example
Company: Publicly Listed Manufacturing Firm
Annual Revenue: $50,000,000
Annual EBITDA: $5,000,000
Market Capitalization: $50,000,000 (10x EBITDA)

Investment Plan
Purchase Price: $50,000,000 (buying shares at market value)
Investor Equity: $50,000,000

Return on Equity
Annual EBITDA: $5,000,000
Net Income (Assuming 20% Tax Rate): $4,000,000
Return on Equity: 8%

Investing in small private businesses offers unique opportunities and challenges compared to investing in listed equities. By understanding valuation multiples, leveraging debt effectively, and adopting a passive investment strategy, investors can achieve significant returns while minimizing active involvement. However, these investments come with higher risk and lower liquidity, requiring careful due diligence and strategic planning.

On the other hand, listed equities provide greater liquidity and stability but often come with higher multiples and limited leverage options. The potential returns are generally lower, but the investment is more accessible and easier to manage for the average investor.

Ultimately, the choice between investing in private businesses and listed equities depends on the investor's goals, risk tolerance, and investment horizon. Both options have their merits and can complement each other in a diversified investment portfolio.

Chapter 2.7
FINANCIAL LITERACY

Essential Knowledge for Investing in Property and Businesses

Investing in property and businesses requires a foundational understanding of several critical areas. While you may not need to become an expert in these fields, having a basic grasp of mathematics, accounting, and law is indispensable. Much like how you don't need to be a master chef to prepare a decent meal, you don't need to be a certified accountant, mathematician, or lawyer to make sound investment decisions. However, knowing the basics can help you navigate the complexities of property and business investments with greater confidence and success.

Mathematics: The Language of Investment

Understanding the Numbers
1. Basic Arithmetic: Addition, subtraction, multiplication, and division are the cornerstones of any investment analysis. You'll use these operations to calculate profits, expenses, returns on investment (ROI), and other essential metrics.
2. Percentages: Understanding percentages is crucial for interpreting interest rates, growth rates, profit margins, and other financial ratios.
3. Compound Interest: This concept is fundamental in calculating the growth of investments over time. It's essential for understanding how your investments will grow due to reinvested earnings.
4. Present Value and Future Value: These calculations help you understand the value of money over time. Present value (PV) helps you determine what future cash flows are worth today, while future value (FV) tells you what an investment made today will be worth in the future.

Practical Applications

- Mortgage Calculations: Determine monthly payments, total interest paid, and the payoff period for loans.
- Investment Growth: Calculate how much an investment will grow over time with a given interest rate.
- ROI Calculations: Measure the profitability of an investment by comparing the gain from the investment to its cost.

Accounting: The Financial Backbone

Key Concepts

1. Financial Statements: Understanding balance sheets, income statements, and cash flow statements is essential. These documents provide a snapshot of a company's financial health.
2. Double-Entry Bookkeeping: This accounting method ensures that the accounting equation (Assets = Liabilities + Equity) always balances. Every transaction affects at least two accounts.
3. Depreciation: Knowing how assets lose value over time and how to account for this in financial statements is crucial for both property and business investments.
4. Taxation: Basic knowledge of tax principles and how they apply to investments can help you make tax-efficient decisions.

Practical Applications

- Evaluating Investments: Analyse financial statements to assess the profitability and stability of potential business investments.
- Budgeting and Forecasting: Prepare budgets and financial forecasts to plan for future expenses and revenues.
- Tax Planning: Understand tax implications and plan your investments to minimize tax liabilities.

Law: Navigating the Legal Landscape

Key Concepts
1. Contracts: Understanding the basics of contract law is crucial for negotiating and drafting agreements. This includes knowing the elements of a valid contract and common terms used in contracts.
2. Property Law: Basic knowledge of property rights, ownership structures, and zoning laws is essential when investing in real estate.
3. Business Law: Familiarity with different business structures (e.g., sole proprietorships, partnerships, corporations) and their legal implications can help you choose the right structure for your investments.
4. Regulations and Compliance: Knowing the regulatory environment for your investments, including securities regulations for publicly traded companies and licensing requirements for businesses, is crucial.

Practical Applications
- Drafting and Reviewing Contracts: Ensure that your investment agreements are legally sound and protect your interests.
- Real Estate Transactions: Navigate the legal aspects of buying, selling, and managing property.
- Business Formation: Choose the right legal structure for your business investments and understand the associated legal responsibilities.

Integrating Knowledge for Investment Success

The Role of Advisors
While having a basic understanding of mathematics, accounting, and law is essential, you don't need to navigate these areas alone. Engaging with professionals such as financial advisors, accountants, and lawyers can provide you with the expertise needed to make informed decisions. However, your foundational

knowledge will enable you to communicate effectively with these professionals and understand their advice.

Continuous Learning

The investment landscape is dynamic, and regulations, market conditions, and financial tools continually evolve. Staying informed through continuous learning, whether through formal education, self-study, or professional development, is crucial. Resources such as online courses, books, and industry seminars can help you stay up-to-date.

Practical Example: Real Estate Investment

Let's consider a practical example of how mathematics, accounting, and law intersect in a real estate investment.

1. Mathematics: You find a property valued at $500,000. Using basic arithmetic, you calculate a 20% down payment of $100,000. You then use compound interest formulas to determine that with an annual mortgage rate of 4%, your monthly payments over 30 years will be approximately $1,910.

2. Accounting: You analyse the property's financial potential by examining its rental income, operating expenses, and potential tax deductions. You prepare a projected income statement showing annual rental income of $30,000, expenses of $10,000, and a net income of $20,000. You account for depreciation to understand its impact on your taxable income.

3. Law: You review the property's title to ensure there are no liens or legal disputes. You draft a lease agreement for potential tenants, ensuring it includes key legal terms such as lease duration, rent amount, and maintenance responsibilities. You also ensure compliance with local zoning laws and rental regulations.

Practical Example: Small Business Investment

Consider investing in a small business.

1. Mathematics: You evaluate a business with annual profits of $100,000, valued at 4 times its profit ($400,000). With a 20% down payment of $80,000 and financing the remaining $320,000, you calculate annual loan repayments and net profits post-repayment.

2. Accounting: You review the business's financial statements, ensuring its balance sheet is strong, and its income statement reflects consistent profitability. You analyze cash flow statements to ensure the business can cover loan repayments.

3. Law: You examine the business's contracts with suppliers and customers, ensuring they are legally sound. You review the business's corporate structure and ensure compliance with industry-specific regulations. You draft an acquisition agreement that outlines the terms of the purchase and protects your interests.

Investing in property and businesses requires a solid foundation in mathematics, accounting, and law. These disciplines provide the tools to analyse investments, understand financial implications, and navigate legal complexities. While you don't need to be an expert, having a basic understanding of these areas is crucial for making informed investment decisions. By integrating this knowledge and leveraging professional advisors, you can enhance your investment strategy and increase your chances of success.

PART 3.
DETAILED ROADMAP

Chapter 3.1
ACHIEVEING MILLIONAIRE STATUS

So now that you know the background based on which the decisions are made, and you understand all the whys, I can show you the how. We've explored the world we live in, our potential within it, and the fundamentals of saving and investing. We've examined the different types of investments and how they function. With all this essential information laid out, you can now logically conclude how to achieve wealth or become a millionaire. So, here's my take on it. The conclusion is simple: save money as soon as you can to start investing. Invest in property and businesses. Period. That is it. That is the whole plan.

To achieve millionaire status in under a decade, it's essential to grasp a comprehensive view of our world, understand the potential we hold, and master the fundamentals of saving and investing. This overview will guide you through the critical components needed to form a sound strategy for wealth accumulation.

First, let's explore the world we live in. We are surrounded by a dynamic economic landscape where opportunities for wealth creation are abundant but competitive. Recognizing this environment is the first step toward leveraging it for financial success.

Understanding who we can be in this world involves acknowledging our potential to influence our financial destiny. The power to change our economic status lies in our hands through disciplined saving and strategic investing.

Saving money is the cornerstone of wealth building. It involves setting aside a portion of your income regularly, which creates the foundation for future investments. Effective saving is not just about putting money aside; it's about developing a mindset of financial prudence and foresight.

When it comes to investments, there are various avenues available, each with its mechanisms and potential returns. These include real estate, where properties can appreciate and generate rental income, and private businesses, where investing can offer high returns but requires careful management and due diligence. Understanding how these investments work is crucial for making informed decisions.

Based on this essential information, the logical conclusion is to begin by saving diligently and investing wisely. The plan is straightforward: start by saving as much as possible and then channel those savings into property and business investments. This approach, while simple, requires breaking it down into manageable steps, which will be detailed in the following sections.

So, now that you have the overview and understand the foundational principles, we can delve into the specifics of how to execute this plan effectively to become wealthy.

Step 1: Saving Money as Soon as Possible

The first step to becoming a millionaire is to start saving money as soon as possible. There are two components to savings: increasing your income and minimizing your expenses.

Increasing Your Income

First, you need to be realistic about your environment. If you live in a third-world country where there are few opportunities to make decent money, it is not impossible to succeed, but it is very hard. As a first step, consider moving to an area that provides higher wages and better potential for a job. This might mean choosing to live in another city or even another country, as many immigrants have successfully done.

You also need to decide whether you will choose a trade occupation and start earning sooner, rather than studying longer for a professional qualification that promises better pay. Be very careful with the word "promises" when it comes to better pay. You need to be sure of why you decided to postpone earning in favour of studying.

In trade occupations, people are usually paid by the hour, and you can work up to 10-12 hours a day and make considerably more money than someone paid a salary that takes into account 8 hours per day. Even though salaried employees might stay at work longer, they are still only paid the contracted yearly amount. You can still choose to study for a professional career and work at the same time. It is hard but doable. This way, you do not miss out on getting the professional qualification but also earn money along the way.

In my opinion, if you are not planning on working your whole life and have it easy by not working too much and still getting a good wage in which case you would choose a professional qualification, but instead you want to build wealth as soon as possible. Then I would choose a trade qualification in order to start earning and saving and investing as soon as I can.

Minimizing Your Expenses

Once you sort out your income, you need to focus on saving that hard-earned money by minimizing your expenses. The main expenses are accommodation, food, transport, entertainment, and travel.

1. Accommodation: The best option is to live with your parents if possible, as this means almost no accommodation expense. The second best is renting a cheap unit and sharing the expenses with a roommate.

2. Food: Do not eat out; prepare food yourself.

3. Transport: It is important to have transport because it gives you the freedom to move easily. You can choose a job that might be hard to get to with public transport or one that you wouldn't feel like going to without personal transport. A personal car lets you enjoy some local travel as well. A 10-year-old car is still in good condition, especially if serviced regularly and has proof of it. Choose a basic, medium-sized 10-year-old car, which would be worth 5-10 low weekly pays in Australia. You can easily get finance for it and slowly repay it over

the next 2-5 years. For example, a $5,000 car financed over 2 years would only cost you about $70 per week.

4. Entertainment: Do not spend money on eating and drinking outside. It is very expensive and unnecessary. An occasional weekend lunch with friends is okay, but there is no need to splurge on it daily or too often.

5. Travel: International travel is very expensive. Do not spend money on it. If you love travel, visit nearby places, national parks, and nearby cities and villages. You probably haven't explored much further than 100 kilometres from where you were raised, or if you move to a new city or country, there is a lot to explore in the new area. Try camping instead of staying in expensive hotels, or at least choose cheap motel accommodation.

Do not act rich if you are not already!

Step 2: Investing in Property

Once you have minimized your expenses, you can start saving the maximum amount. The first thing you should invest in is property. Do not buy your dream property; buy the cheapest property you can and make double the minimum loan repayments.

In Australia, in Sydney in 2024, you can get a one-bedroom apartment for $350,000. As a first property, you only need to save up 10% of its value to get finance for it, which would equate to $35,000. Once you buy it, keep making double repayments until your equity (the repaid amount) is equal to 20% of the next property. Then, rent out the first property and repeat the process. Continue this cycle for the next 10 years or more.

Step 3: Investing in Businesses

Once you have a couple of properties, you can start investing in businesses, which are riskier investments but can also be very rewarding. Most financiers (banks or other non-bank financing institutions) require a 20% deposit for the purchase of a business.

Choose a low-value business; in Australia, this could mean businesses worth $100,000 to $200,000, for which you would need only a $20,000 to $40,000 deposit. If these businesses are profitable (as they should be), with a minimum 20% return, they will cover your loans. After 5 years, you will have a business worth $100,000 to $200,000. So, your equity grew from $20,000 to $100,000. Now, repeat this process over the next few years with new savings or extra cash from businesses and watch your wealth grow.

To achieve a millionaire status, you need a clear and disciplined approach. Start by saving money as soon as possible by increasing your income and minimizing your expenses. Invest in property as your first step, and once you have a couple of properties, start investing in businesses. Continuously educate yourself, particularly in accounting and business management, to maximize your returns and manage your investments effectively.

Remember, the key to success is to take action and stay committed to your plan. With perseverance and smart decision-making, you can achieve financial independence and become a millionaire.

Chapter 3.2
INCREASING YOUR INCOME

One of the most crucial steps towards becoming a millionaire in ten years is increasing your income. While this may sound straightforward, it requires careful planning, strategic decisions, and unwavering dedication. This chapter explores the avenues through which you can enhance your earnings, the importance of making those earnings count, and the realities of different career paths.

Working While Studying

Many people make the mistake of working while studying but then spending all the money they earn. This approach defeats the purpose of working in the first place. The goal should be to make that hard-earned cash count towards your ultimate goal – investing. Whether you are in a trade occupation or pursuing a professional career, the income you generate during your studies should be saved and invested wisely.

Trade Occupations: Start Earning Early

Choosing a trade occupation can allow you to start earning at an early age. Trades such as plumbing, electrical work, carpentry, and other skilled labor offer the opportunity to begin making money soon after completing vocational training. Here's how you can leverage this path:

1. Early Entry into the Workforce: Trade occupations typically require shorter training periods compared to professional careers. This means you can start earning good money by the age of 18.

2. Potential for Long Hours: Tradespeople often have the flexibility to work longer hours, increasing their weekly earnings. This can be particularly beneficial if you are focused on saving and investing a significant portion of your income.

3. Entrepreneurial Opportunities: After gaining experience, you may have the potential to open your own business. By the age of 22, if you are capable and driven

enough to attract and retain clients, you can transition from being an employee to a business owner. However, it's important to acknowledge the reality – approximately 80% of people may struggle with this transition due to fear or a lack of motivation.

Professional Careers: Delayed Gratification

If you pursue a professional career, your journey will look different but can still lead to significant earnings. Here's a breakdown of the typical path:
1. Studying and Earning: Starting at 18, you will focus on your studies, possibly working part-time to support yourself. The key here is to save and invest the money you earn from part-time jobs rather than spending it all.
2. Graduation and Entry-Level Positions: By the age of 22, if everything goes well, you will complete your studies and enter the workforce in a junior position. While the initial salary might not be as high as in trade occupations, the potential for growth is substantial.
3. Potential for Business Ownership: If you are capable, you could potentially open your own business by the age of 26 or 28. However, similar to trade occupations, the reality is that about 80% of individuals might not pursue this path due to fear or lack of motivation.

Making Your Earnings Count

Regardless of the path you choose, the key to increasing your income effectively is to ensure that your earnings are not wasted. Here are some strategies to help you maximize the impact of your income:
1. Save a Significant Portion of Your Income: Aim to save at least 20-30% of your income. This might require making sacrifices in the short term, but the long-term benefits are substantial.

2. Invest Wisely: Use your savings to invest in assets that appreciate over time, such as property and private businesses. The earlier you start investing, the more time your money has to grow.

3. Avoid Lifestyle Inflation: As your income increases, resist the temptation to inflate your lifestyle. Keep your expenses in check and continue to save and invest aggressively.

Overcoming Barriers to Success

While the strategies mentioned above are straightforward, they are not easy to implement. Many people face barriers such as fear, lack of motivation, and a tendency to procrastinate. Here are some tips to overcome these challenges:

1. Set Clear Goals: Having clear, achievable goals can help keep you motivated. Write down your financial goals and review them regularly to stay focused.

2. Educate Yourself: Continuous learning is essential. Read books, attend seminars, and seek mentorship to enhance your knowledge about saving, investing, and business management.

3. Build a Support System: Surround yourself with like-minded individuals who can support and motivate you. This could be friends, family, or a mentor who shares your vision and can offer guidance.

The Reality Check

It's important to acknowledge that not everyone will succeed in significantly increasing their income or transitioning to business ownership. The reality is that approximately 80% of people may struggle with fear or lack of motivation. However, recognizing this statistic should not deter you. Instead, use it as a motivator to push beyond the average and strive for excellence.

Conclusion

Increasing your income is a pivotal step in your journey to becoming a millionaire in ten years. Whether you choose a trade occupation or a professional career, the principles remain the same: start earning early, save and invest wisely, and remain disciplined and motivated. By making your earnings count and overcoming barriers to success, you can significantly enhance your financial prospects and move closer to your goal of financial independence. Remember, the path is challenging, but with dedication and strategic planning, it is achievable.

Chapter 3.3
MINIMIZING YOUR EXPENSES

Accommodation

Minimizing your expenses is a critical component of your journey to becoming a millionaire in ten years. By reducing your outgoings, you can save a significant portion of your income, which can then be channelled into investments. One of the most substantial expenses for most people is accommodation. Here are some strategies to help you minimize your accommodation costs effectively.

Live with Your Parents

If possible, living with your parents is the best way to save on accommodation expenses. This option provides several benefits:

1. No Rent: By living with your parents, you eliminate rent payments entirely, allowing you to save a substantial portion of your income.

2. Reduced Utility Costs: Typically, living at home means lower or no utility bills, further reducing your monthly expenses.

3. Support System: Staying with your parents can provide emotional and logistical support, which can be invaluable as you focus on building your financial future.

While this option might not be feasible for everyone, it's worth considering if your family dynamics allow for it. The money saved by not paying rent can be a significant boost to your savings and investment funds.

Rent with Roommates

If living with your parents is not an option, consider renting a place with roommates. Sharing a rental property can drastically reduce your accommodation costs. Here's how:

1. Shared Rent: Splitting the rent with one or more roommates reduces the amount each person has to pay. This can make living in a desirable area more affordable.

2. Shared Utilities: Utility bills such as electricity, water, and internet can also be divided among roommates, further decreasing individual expenses.

3. Shared Household Items: Costs for household items like furniture, kitchen supplies, and cleaning products can be shared, reducing the overall expenditure for each person.

Living with roommates requires compromise and good communication, but the financial benefits can make it a worthwhile arrangement. It's important to choose roommates who are reliable and have similar financial goals to avoid potential conflicts.

Rent and Sublet

Another effective strategy is to rent an entire apartment and sublet other rooms. This approach allows you to take on the role of a landlord in a small way, potentially reducing or even eliminating your own rent costs. Here's how it works:

1. Rent the Entire Property: Find a reasonably priced apartment with multiple bedrooms. Ensure the total rent is within a manageable range for your income level.

2. Sublet Rooms: Sublet the extra rooms to tenants. The rent you charge should cover the majority, if not all, of the total rent you pay to the landlord.

3. Live Rent-Free or at a Discount: If done correctly, the income from your subtenants can significantly offset your rent, allowing you to live for free or at a much-reduced cost.

Before pursuing this option, make sure to check local laws and your lease agreement to ensure subletting is allowed. Additionally, carefully select your subtenants to avoid any potential issues.

Additional Tips for Minimizing Accommodation Costs

1. Negotiate Rent: When signing a lease, don't hesitate to negotiate the rent with your landlord. They may be willing to lower the rent slightly to secure a reliable tenant.

2. Choose a Location Wisely: Opt for locations that are slightly further from city centers but still accessible. These areas tend to have lower rent prices while still providing necessary amenities.

3. Maintain the Property: Taking good care of the rental property can help you avoid additional costs. Landlords are more likely to return your security deposit if the property is well-maintained, and you might avoid extra charges for damages.

Minimizing your accommodation expenses is a powerful way to boost your savings and accelerate your journey to becoming a millionaire. Whether you live with your parents, share a rental with roommates, or sublet rooms, the key is to keep your costs as low as possible. By implementing these strategies, you can free up more of your income for saving and investing, bringing you one step closer to achieving financial independence. Remember, every dollar saved is a dollar that can work for you in your investments, helping you build wealth over time.

Minimize Your Expenses – Food

Minimizing your food expenses is a key strategy in saving money to invest in your future. By preparing your meals at home, buying in bulk, and choosing cost-effective ingredients, you can significantly reduce your food costs. Here's how to do it effectively.

Prepare Your Food Yourself

One of the simplest ways to save money on food is by preparing your meals at home. Cooking your own meals not only allows you to control what you eat but also helps you save a significant amount of money compared to eating out. Here are some tips:

1. Plan Your Meals: Take some time each week to plan your meals. This helps you avoid last-minute takeout and ensures you have all the ingredients you need.

2. Cook in Batches: Prepare large quantities of food and store them in the refrigerator or freezer. This can save you time and ensure you have meals ready to go when you're busy.

3. Use Simple Recipes: Stick to simple, easy-to-follow recipes that don't require a lot of expensive ingredients or elaborate preparation.

Buy in Bulk

Buying groceries in bulk can lead to substantial savings. Bulk items often cost less per unit than smaller packages, and having a stockpile of essential ingredients can help you avoid frequent trips to the store. Here's how to make the most of bulk buying:

1. Focus on Staples: Stock up on staple foods like rice, pasta, beans, and oats. These items have a long shelf life and can be used in a variety of dishes.

2. Buy Meat in Bulk: Purchase larger cuts of meat or bulk packs when they're on sale. Divide them into smaller portions and freeze what you won't use immediately.

3. Store Properly: Make sure to store bulk items properly to prevent spoilage. Use airtight containers for dry goods and freezer bags for meats and other perishables.

Eat Cheap Meat Cuts

When it comes to protein, choosing cheaper cuts of meat can save you a lot of money. These cuts are often just as nutritious and can be made tender and flavorful with the right cooking methods. Consider the following:

1. Use Slow Cooking Methods: Cheaper cuts of meat, like chuck roast or pork shoulder, can be tough, but slow cooking them in a crockpot or braising them can make them tender and delicious.

2. Ground Meat: Ground beef, turkey, or chicken is often more affordable than whole cuts and can be used in a variety of dishes.

3. Offal: Organ meats like liver and kidneys are usually much cheaper than muscle cuts and are packed with nutrients.

Stick to Healthy Whole Foods

Focusing on healthy, whole foods can help you maintain a balanced diet while keeping costs down. Prioritize protein sources like eggs, meats, and dairy, and complement them with affordable carbs and produce. Here's a breakdown:

1. Proteins: Eggs, milk, yogurt, and cheese are cost-effective protein sources. They can be used in many different recipes and provide essential nutrients.

2. Carbohydrates: Bread, rice, potatoes, and pasta are inexpensive and versatile. They can be the base for many meals, helping to stretch your food budget further.

3. Fruits and Vegetables: While some produce can be expensive, there are plenty of affordable options like bananas, apples, carrots, and cabbage. Buying in-season produce can also reduce costs.

Avoid Eating Out

Eating out, even at fast food restaurants like McDonald's, can quickly drain your budget. The cost of a single meal out could provide ingredients for several home-cooked meals. Here's why you should avoid eating out frequently:

1. Cost Comparison: A meal at McDonald's might seem cheap, but for the same price, you could prepare multiple meals at home. For example, the cost of a fast-food combo meal could cover the ingredients for three home-cooked meals.

2. Healthier Choices: Home-cooked meals are typically healthier than fast food. You have control over the ingredients and can avoid excess salt, sugar, and unhealthy fats.

3. Effort and Planning: Yes, cooking takes time and effort, but the financial savings and health benefits are worth it. Plan your grocery shopping and meal prep to streamline the process.

Minimizing your food expenses is a crucial step in maximizing your savings and investing in your future. By preparing your meals at home, buying in bulk, choosing cheaper cuts of meat, and sticking to whole foods, you can significantly reduce your food costs. Avoiding the convenience of eating out and committing to cooking your own meals will require some effort and planning, but the financial rewards will make it worthwhile. Remember, every dollar saved on food is a dollar that can be invested towards achieving your goal of becoming a millionaire in ten years.

Minimize Your Expenses – Transport

When considering how to minimize your expenses, transportation is a crucial area to address. Owning a car can provide significant benefits, including increased freedom of movement and the ability to take on jobs that would be inaccessible with public transport. However, it's essential to manage this expense wisely. Here's how to do it.

<u>The Necessity of Owning a Car</u>

Having a car gives you the freedom to move around easily and take advantage of job opportunities that might not be accessible via public transport. This flexibility can save you considerable time and increase your earning potential. However, owning a car comes with costs that need to be carefully managed to avoid financial strain.

Calculating the Costs

Just to own a car, excluding the purchase price, you need to consider several ongoing expenses:

1. Petrol: On average, you might spend about $50 per week on petrol, which adds up to $2,500 per year.
2. Yearly Registration: In many places, car registration costs around $500 per year.
3. Insurance: Basic insurance typically costs about $500 per year.
4. Service and Maintenance: Regular servicing and maintenance also average around $500 per year.

In total, these expenses amount to approximately $4,000 per year.

If you are considering the purchase price of the car, let's assume you finance a $10,000 car over five years. This adds about $2,000 per year, bringing the total annual cost to $6,000.

Choosing the Right Car

Opting for a used car rather than a new one can save you a substantial amount of money. For example, a new Toyota Corolla might cost around $30,000. However, due to depreciation, its value halves approximately every five years. So, a five-year-old Corolla might cost $15,000, and a ten-year-old model could be as low as $7,500.

These cars are generally reliable, especially if they have been serviced regularly. Ensure that the car you are considering has a service book to confirm its maintenance history. Expect to replace parts that wear out over time, such as tires, brakes, and batteries, but these are manageable costs.

Financing Your Car Purchase

It's advisable not to buy a car outright with cash. Financing the purchase over a period (such as five years) can be more financially prudent. Here's why:

1. Preserve Your Cash for Investments: Cash is better used for investments rather than paying for a depreciating asset. Use your cash to invest in assets that appreciate over time.

2. Manageable Payments: Financing a car means you spread the cost over several years, which aligns with how you pay for other expenses like food, property, and clothing. This approach helps manage your cash flow more effectively.
For instance, if the additional cost of financing is $2,000 per year, as previously mentioned, it's a relatively small part of your total annual car expenses ($6,000). Therefore, it makes sense to finance rather than spend a lump sum upfront.

Practical Tips for Minimizing Car Expenses
1. Buy a Reliable Used Car: As highlighted, cars like the Toyota Corolla are affordable, reliable, and have a good resale value. Ensure the car has a full service history.
2. Regular Maintenance: Keep your car well-maintained to avoid costly repairs. Regular oil changes, tire rotations, and other basic maintenance can extend the life of your car.
3. Consider Fuel Efficiency: Choose a car with good fuel efficiency to save on petrol costs. Smaller cars usually consume less fuel.
4. Shop Around for Insurance: Compare insurance rates to get the best deal. Ensure you have adequate coverage without overpaying.
5. Drive Responsibly: Avoid aggressive driving, which can increase fuel consumption and wear on the car. Adhering to speed limits and driving smoothly can reduce maintenance costs.

Owning a car is a significant expense, but it can also be a valuable tool for increasing your earning potential and improving your quality of life. By choosing a reliable used car, financing the purchase, and managing ongoing costs, you can minimize the financial impact of car ownership. Remember, a car is an expense, not an asset, so it's essential to manage it as such. Use your cash for investments that appreciate over time and pay for your car as you go. This strategy will help you achieve your financial goals without compromising your mobility and freedom.

Guide to Millions

Minimize Your Expenses – Entertainment

Entertainment is an essential part of life, but it can also be a significant drain on your finances if not managed wisely. By making conscious choices about how you entertain yourself and socialize, you can enjoy a rich and fulfilling social life without breaking the bank. Here are some strategies to minimize your entertainment expenses.

Reevaluate Party Venues

      One of the biggest expenses when it comes to entertainment is going out to expensive venues. Nightclubs, bars, and fancy restaurants can quickly drain your wallet. Instead of spending large amounts of money on cover charges, overpriced drinks, and meals, consider alternative ways to socialize and have fun.

Host Home Gatherings

      Hosting gatherings at home is a fantastic way to save money while still enjoying the company of friends and family. You can create a cozy and inviting atmosphere without the high costs associated with going out. Here are a few tips for successful home gatherings:

1. Potluck Dinners: Ask each guest to bring a dish. This way, you can enjoy a variety of foods without bearing the entire cost yourself.
2. BYOB: Encourage guests to bring their own beverages. This reduces the cost of providing drinks for everyone and ensures there's something everyone will enjoy.
3. Themed Nights: Host themed nights such as game nights, movie marathons, or karaoke sessions. This adds an element of fun and excitement without extra costs.

Utilize Public Spaces

If you prefer not to host at home or if your space is limited, consider using public spaces for gatherings. Parks, beaches, and lakes offer beautiful and cost-effective settings for social events. Here's how to make the most of these venues:
1. Picnics: Organize a picnic where everyone brings a dish or snacks. You can enjoy the outdoors and good company without spending a fortune.
2. Outdoor Games: Bring along some sports equipment like frisbees, soccer balls, or badminton sets. These activities are free and great for bonding.
3. Barbecues: Many parks have barbecue facilities that you can use. Grilling outdoors is a fun and inexpensive way to enjoy a meal with friends.

Strengthen Friendships
One of the best ways to enhance your social life without spending a lot of money is to strengthen your friendships. Building a close-knit group of friends can provide a strong support network and make socializing more enjoyable and cost-effective.
1. Organize Regular Meetups: Establish a routine where you and your friends meet regularly at each other's homes or in public spaces. This creates a sense of tradition and reduces the need for costly outings.
2. Share Responsibilities: Take turns hosting events or planning activities. This distributes the costs and effort, making it easier for everyone to participate.
3. Leverage Friend Networks: It's often easier and more comfortable to meet new people through mutual friends rather than approaching strangers in public venues. Expanding your social circle through existing connections can lead to meaningful relationships and enjoyable social experiences without additional costs.

Mindful Spending on Entertainment
Even when you do decide to go out, there are ways to keep your expenses in check:
1. Happy Hours: Take advantage of happy hour deals at bars and restaurants. You can enjoy discounts on food and drinks during these times.

2. Discounts and Coupons: Look for discounts, coupons, and deals for movies, concerts, and other entertainment activities. Many websites and apps offer great deals on tickets and events.

3. Free Events: Keep an eye out for free events in your community, such as festivals, concerts in the park, or art exhibitions. These can be enjoyable and enriching experiences that don't cost anything.

4. Set a Budget: Allocate a specific amount for entertainment each month and stick to it. This helps you keep track of your spending and ensures you don't overspend.

Minimizing your entertainment expenses doesn't mean sacrificing your social life or the quality of your leisure time. By making thoughtful choices and exploring alternative ways to entertain yourself and your friends, you can enjoy a rich and fulfilling social life without the financial burden. Hosting home gatherings, utilizing public spaces, and strengthening friendships are all effective strategies to maintain an active social life while keeping costs low. Remember, the key to financial success is not just about earning more but also about spending wisely. By applying these principles to your entertainment expenses, you can save money and still have a great time.

Minimize Your Expenses – Travel

Traveling can be one of the most enriching experiences in life, but it can also be one of the most expensive. However, there are many ways to enjoy the benefits of travel without incurring high costs. By making smart choices about where you go, how you get there, and where you stay, you can explore new places and create wonderful memories while keeping your expenses in check. Here are some strategies to minimize your travel expenses.

<u>Avoid International Travel</u>

International travel can be very costly due to high expenses associated with plane tickets and accommodation. Prices often surge during peak travel seasons, such as summer and school holidays, making it even more expensive. Instead of spending a large portion of your budget on international trips, consider exploring your own country or neighbouring countries. Domestic travel can offer just as much adventure and discovery without the hefty price tag.

Explore Your Local Area

Now that you have a car, you have the freedom to explore the areas close to home. Local travel can be incredibly rewarding and provide unique experiences that you might overlook otherwise. Here are a few ways to make the most of local travel:

1. Day Trips: Plan day trips to nearby towns, nature reserves, or tourist attractions. This allows you to explore new places without the need for overnight accommodation.
2. Weekend Getaways: Take advantage of long weekends to visit destinations within driving distance. You can discover charming villages, scenic landscapes, and cultural landmarks without spending a fortune.
3. Hidden Gems: Research lesser-known destinations that are off the beaten path. These places are often more affordable and less crowded, offering a more authentic travel experience.

Camping

One of the best ways to minimize travel expenses is by camping instead of staying in hotels. Camping allows you to immerse yourself in nature and enjoy the great outdoors while saving money on accommodation. Here are some tips for successful camping trips:

1. Invest in Gear: Purchase quality camping gear that will last for multiple trips. A good tent, sleeping bag, and cooking equipment can make your camping experience comfortable and enjoyable.

2. Campgrounds: Look for campgrounds in national parks, state parks, and other scenic areas. These sites are usually affordable and offer beautiful surroundings.
3. Plan Ahead: Reserve your campsite in advance, especially during peak seasons. This ensures you get a spot and helps you plan your trip better.

Stay in Cheap Motels

If camping is not your style or if you prefer more comfort, consider staying in cheap motels instead of expensive hotels. Motels can provide a comfortable place to rest without the high costs associated with luxury accommodations. Here are some ways to find affordable motels:
1. Search Online: Use travel websites and apps to compare prices and read reviews. This helps you find the best deals and avoid low-quality accommodations.
2. Off-Peak Travel: Travel during off-peak times when motel rates are lower. Avoid holidays and weekends when prices tend to be higher.
3. Loyalty Programs: Join motel loyalty programs to earn points and receive discounts on future stays. Many chains offer these programs, which can lead to significant savings over time.

Explore Neighbouring Countries by Car

If you want to venture beyond your own country, consider exploring neighbouring countries by car. Driving allows you to control your travel expenses and gives you the flexibility to explore at your own pace. Here are some tips for international road trips:
1. Plan Your Route: Research your route and plan your stops in advance. This helps you budget for fuel, tolls, and accommodation.
2. Cross-Border Travel: Check the requirements for crossing borders, such as visas, insurance, and vehicle documentation. Make sure you have everything in order before you leave.
3. Local Cuisine: Instead of dining in expensive restaurants, try local eateries and street food. This not only saves money but also gives you a taste of the local culture.

Make the Most of Your Travel Budget

Traveling on a budget doesn't mean you have to sacrifice fun or comfort. By making smart choices and planning ahead, you can enjoy memorable travel experiences without overspending. Here are a few additional tips to maximize your travel budget:

1. Pack Wisely: Bring everything you need to avoid buying items at your destination, where they might be more expensive. This includes snacks, toiletries, and entertainment.
2. Local Experiences: Engage in free or low-cost activities such as hiking, visiting museums on free admission days, or exploring local markets. These experiences can be just as rewarding as expensive tours and excursions.
3. Travel Light: Pack light to avoid extra baggage fees if you're flying or to make your car journey more comfortable and fuel-efficient.

Minimizing your travel expenses is about making thoughtful choices and prioritizing experiences over luxury. By avoiding costly international travel, exploring local areas, camping, staying in affordable motels, and planning budget-friendly road trips, you can enjoy the benefits of travel without the financial strain. Remember, the goal is to create lasting memories and enrich your life without compromising your financial stability. With careful planning and a bit of creativity, you can travel far and wide while keeping your expenses in check.

Example of Savings Potential for a Junior Electrician Based on Sydney Prices in 2024

Understanding the potential for savings is crucial for anyone aiming to build wealth. Let's delve into an example of a junior electrician's income and expenses in Sydney in 2024 to highlight how effective budgeting and expense management can significantly impact savings.

Income

A junior electrician in Sydney earns approximately $35 per hour. Tradespeople often work long hours and can benefit from working on Saturdays to maximize their income. Here's a breakdown of the weekly earnings for a junior electrician working 10 hours a day, 6 days a week:

- Hourly rate: $35
- Daily income: $35 x 10 hours = $350
- Weekly income: $350 x 6 days = $2,100

Weekly Expenses

To understand the savings potential, we need to consider the weekly expenses a junior electrician might incur. These expenses include rent, food, clothing, car-related costs, entertainment, and travel. Below are two scenarios: one living with parents and the other living with a roommate.

Scenario 1: Living with Parents
1. Rent: $0
2. Food: $200
3. Clothing: $50
4. Car: $150
5. Entertainment: $200 (coffee, drinks, pizza)
6. Travel: $100 (average annual travel cost spread weekly)
- Total weekly expenses: $700

Scenario 2: Living with a Roommate
1. Rent: $300
2. Food: $200
3. Clothing: $50
4. Car: $150

5. Entertainment: $200 (coffee, drinks, pizza)
6. Travel: $100 (average annual travel cost spread weekly)
- Total weekly expenses: $1,000

Savings Potential

With the income and expenses outlined, let's calculate the weekly and annual savings for both scenarios.

Savings with Parents:
- Weekly savings: $2,100 (income) - $700 (expenses) = $1,400
- Annual savings**: $1,400 x 50 weeks = $70,000

Savings without Parents:
- Weekly savings: $2,100 (income) - $1,000 (expenses) = $1,100
- Annual savings: $1,100 x 50 weeks = $55,000

<u>Maximizing Savings</u>

To maximize savings, a junior electrician should focus on increasing income and minimizing expenses. Here are some strategies:

1. Chase Overtime Opportunities: Tradespeople often have opportunities for overtime. If your current employer doesn't offer it, seek out companies that do. Working additional hours can significantly boost your income.

2. Live Frugally: Living with parents can dramatically reduce expenses, allowing for higher savings. If that's not possible, sharing a rental property with roommates is the next best option.

3. Budget for Essentials: Allocate a fixed amount for essential expenses such as food, clothing, and transportation. Avoid unnecessary spending and prioritize saving.

4. Control Entertainment Costs: Socializing and entertainment are important, but they don't have to be expensive. Limit spending on coffee, drinks, and dining out. Organize budget-friendly gatherings with friends to keep costs low.

5. Plan Travel Wisely: Travel is a valuable experience, but it should be done within budget. Opt for local travel or affordable destinations to keep travel expenses manageable.

6. Car Expenses: Owning a car is often necessary for tradespeople, but choose a reliable, used car to keep purchase costs down. Regular maintenance can prevent costly repairs in the long run.

Long-Term Impact

The savings potential for a junior electrician in Sydney is substantial. By following a disciplined approach to income generation and expense management, significant savings can be accumulated over time. For example, saving $70,000 annually while living with parents or $55,000 annually while living with a roommate can provide a strong financial foundation.

These savings can be invested in assets such as property or private businesses, which are crucial steps in the journey to becoming a millionaire. Starting early, maintaining a high savings rate, and making wise investment choices are the keys to financial success.

A junior electrician in Sydney has the potential to save a significant amount of money by managing expenses wisely and maximizing income through overtime opportunities. By living frugally and making informed financial decisions, substantial savings can be accumulated, providing a solid foundation for future investments. This disciplined approach to savings and expense management is a critical component of building wealth and achieving financial independence.

Chapter 3.4
INVEST IN PROPERTY

Start with Your Own House – Eliminating Your Biggest Expense: Rent

One of the most impactful strategies for building wealth through property investment is starting with your own home. Owning your own house not only provides you with a stable living situation but also eliminates your biggest recurring expense—rent. This chapter will explore the benefits of buying your own home, the financial advantages, and the steps to take to make this significant investment.

The Financial Impact of Rent

Rent is often the largest monthly expense for most people. In Sydney, for instance, the average rent for a one-bedroom apartment can range from $300 to $600 per week, depending on the location. Over a year, this translates to $15,600 to $31,200. Over a decade, these figures become even more staggering—$156,000 to $312,000. This money, spent on rent, essentially disappears without contributing to your long-term financial security or building equity.

Building Equity with Home Ownership

When you buy a house, you start building equity—a financial asset that represents ownership value. Each mortgage payment contributes to this equity, unlike rent payments that go to the landlord. Equity increases over time as you pay down your mortgage and as property values rise. This growing equity can be leveraged for future investments, such as buying additional properties or starting a business.

Mortgage Payments vs. Rent

While buying a house requires a significant initial investment, including a down payment and closing costs, mortgage payments often compare favourably to rent payments. For example, with current interest rates and a modest down payment, the monthly mortgage payment for a $500,000 home could be around

$2,500. This is comparable to or even less than what you might pay in rent for a similar property in a desirable location. Additionally, mortgage payments remain relatively stable over time, whereas rent can increase annually.

Tax Benefits

Homeownership comes with several tax advantages. Mortgage interest and property taxes are often deductible on your income tax return, reducing your taxable income. These deductions can amount to significant savings, particularly in the early years of a mortgage when interest payments are highest.

Steps to Buying Your First Home

1. Assess Your Financial Situation: Before buying a home, evaluate your financial health. This includes checking your credit score, assessing your savings for a down payment, and understanding your debt-to-income ratio. A good credit score and a low debt-to-income ratio will help you secure a favourable mortgage rate.

2. Save for a Down Payment: A down payment is typically 10-20% of the home's purchase price. For a $500,000 home, this means saving $50,000 to $100,000. Start saving early, and consider setting up a dedicated savings account for your down payment.

3. Get Pre-Approved for a Mortgage: A mortgage pre-approval gives you a clear picture of how much you can afford to spend on a home. It also shows sellers that you are a serious buyer. Shop around for mortgage rates and terms from different lenders to find the best deal.

4. Determine Your Budget: Consider not only the purchase price of the home but also other costs such as property taxes, insurance, maintenance, and utilities. Ensure that your monthly housing costs do not exceed 30% of your gross monthly income.

5. Find the Right Property: Work with a real estate agent to find a home that meets your needs and fits your budget. Consider factors such as location, size, condition, and potential for appreciation.

6. Make an Offer and Close the Deal: Once you find the right home, make an offer. Your real estate agent will help you negotiate the price and terms. After your offer is accepted, you will enter the closing process, which includes securing your mortgage, getting a home inspection, and signing the final paperwork.

Long-Term Benefits of Home Ownership

1. Stability and Security: Owning a home provides stability and a sense of security. You are not subject to the whims of a landlord or potential rent increases. This stability can be particularly beneficial for families with children, as it allows them to stay in one school district and build a strong community network.

2. Appreciation: Real estate typically appreciates over time. While there can be fluctuations in the market, the long-term trend has been upward. This means that your home will likely increase in value, building your net worth.

3. Forced Savings: A mortgage payment is a form of forced savings. Each payment reduces your principal balance and increases your equity. This disciplined approach to saving can be more effective than relying on personal savings alone.

4. Leveraging Equity: The equity you build in your home can be leveraged for other investments. Home equity loans or lines of credit allow you to borrow against the value of your home, often at lower interest rates than other types of loans. This can provide capital for starting a business, investing in additional properties, or funding major expenses such as education or home improvements.

Overcoming Common Obstacles

1. High Initial Costs: The initial costs of buying a home, including the down payment, closing costs, and moving expenses, can be daunting. To overcome this, start saving early and consider first-time homebuyer programs that offer grants, low-interest loans, or assistance with down payments and closing costs.

2. Market Fluctuations: The real estate market can be unpredictable. While long-term trends are generally positive, short-term fluctuations can be challenging. To mitigate this risk, buy a home with the intention of staying for at least

five to seven years. This timeframe allows you to ride out potential downturns in the market.

3. Maintenance and Repairs: Owning a home comes with the responsibility of maintenance and repairs. Budget for these expenses by setting aside 1-2% of your home's value each year for upkeep. Regular maintenance can prevent small issues from becoming major problems.

Starting with your own house is a powerful strategy for eliminating your biggest expense—rent—and building a solid financial foundation. Homeownership offers numerous benefits, including equity building, tax advantages, stability, and long-term appreciation. By carefully assessing your financial situation, saving for a down payment, and making informed decisions throughout the home-buying process, you can turn your home into a valuable asset that supports your journey to financial independence and wealth accumulation.

You Don't Need to Live Where You Buy

In the realm of property investing, one of the most empowering realizations is that you don't necessarily need to live in the properties you purchase. In fact, many successful investors own properties far from where they reside. However, living in your investment property for the first year can offer several strategic advantages. This chapter will explore the reasons behind this approach and how it can benefit your overall investment strategy.

Understanding Property Investment Flexibility

Investing in real estate is all about flexibility and leveraging opportunities wherever they arise. The primary goal is to find properties that offer the best potential for appreciation, rental income, or both. These opportunities might not always be in your immediate vicinity. Here's why:

1. Market Variability: Real estate markets vary significantly from one location to another. A savvy investor looks for markets with high growth potential, favorable economic conditions, and attractive rental yields. This might mean investing in a different city, state, or even country.

2. Diversification: Just as with other forms of investment, diversification is key in real estate. Owning properties in various locations spreads your risk. If one market experiences a downturn, your portfolio remains protected by properties in more stable or prosperous areas.

3. Affordability: Sometimes, the best investment opportunities are in locations where property prices are more affordable compared to where you live. Lower entry costs can provide higher returns on investment and allow you to purchase more properties.

Benefits of Living in Your Investment Property Initially

While you don't need to live where you buy, doing so for the first year can offer numerous benefits:

1. Owner-Occupant Loans: Many lenders offer favourable mortgage rates and terms for owner-occupied properties compared to investment properties. By living in the property initially, you can take advantage of these better rates, which can significantly reduce your mortgage costs.

2. Tax Advantages: Owner-occupants can access various tax benefits, including deductions on mortgage interest and property taxes. These deductions can lower your taxable income, providing substantial savings.

3. First-Hand Knowledge: Living in the property allows you to gain first-hand experience with the home and the neighbourhood. This insight is invaluable when you eventually rent it out, as you can address potential issues before tenants move in and provide accurate descriptions of the property's features and the area's amenities.

4. Improvements and Renovations: As a resident, you'll have the opportunity to make improvements and renovations that can increase the property's

value and rental appeal. Being on-site makes it easier to oversee projects and ensure quality workmanship.

5. Rental Income Potential: By living in the property first, you can assess its rental income potential based on your experience. You'll have a better understanding of what tenants might value and be willing to pay for, helping you set competitive rental rates.

Steps to Take When Living in Your Investment Property

If you decide to live in your investment property for the first year, here are the steps to take to maximize the benefits:

1. Secure an Owner-Occupant Loan: When applying for a mortgage, ensure you disclose your intention to live in the property. This will qualify you for owner-occupant loan terms. Remember, most lenders require you to live in the property for at least a year to maintain these favorable terms.

2. Understand Tax Implications: Consult with a tax professional to understand the specific tax benefits available to owner-occupants. They can help you maximize deductions and ensure compliance with tax regulations.

3. Conduct a Thorough Inspection: Before moving in, conduct a thorough inspection of the property. Address any immediate repairs and create a plan for any necessary renovations or improvements.

4. Immerse Yourself in the Community: Take time to explore the neighborhood. Understand the local amenities, schools, transportation options, and community activities. This knowledge will be useful when marketing the property to potential tenants.

Living in your investment property for the first year is a strategic move that can provide numerous financial and practical benefits. While real estate investing inherently offers flexibility and the ability to capitalize on diverse market opportunities, starting with an owner-occupied property can set a solid foundation for your investment journey. By securing better loan terms, leveraging tax advantages, gaining intimate knowledge of the property and neighbourhood, overseeing improvements, and accurately gauging rental potential, you position yourself for long-term success.

Remember, the initial year of living in your investment property is a time to lay the groundwork for a profitable future. Embrace the opportunity to enhance the property's value, familiarize yourself with the community, and prepare it for future tenants. This approach not only maximizes your investment returns but also provides a seamless transition into the life of a property investor.

Ultimately, the decision to live in your investment property initially should be seen as a strategic step rather than a necessity. Once you've reaped the benefits of this initial phase, you can confidently expand your portfolio, exploring new markets and diversifying your investments. By taking this calculated approach, you harness the full potential of real estate investing, paving the way to financial independence and success.

Discovering The Ideal Investment Property

Investing in property can be a powerful strategy for building wealth, but identifying a good investment property requires a thorough understanding of both external and internal factors that drive successful investments. The journey to finding the perfect investment property involves assessing its surroundings and context as well as evaluating its potential for capital growth, cashflow, and yield. Here's a comprehensive guide to discovering the ideal investment property.

External Factors: Assessing the Property's Context
1. Affordability

Affordability is a crucial external factor when evaluating potential investment properties. The first step is to align your property investment with your current income levels and financial capabilities. This means choosing properties that are within your budget, considering not just the purchase price but also ongoing expenses such as maintenance, property taxes, and insurance. Avoid stretching your finances too thin; instead, aim for properties that offer a balance between cost and potential return.

2. Lifestyle Preferences

Today's property market is shaped by lifestyle preferences, which significantly influence property demand. Look for properties in locations that cater to contemporary living preferences, such as proximity to schools, parks, recreational facilities, and shopping centers. Properties that align with current lifestyle trends are likely to attract tenants and buyers, ensuring sustained demand and rental income. For example, properties near vibrant community hubs or those offering modern amenities tend to be more appealing.

3. Infrastructure Developments

Proximity to major infrastructure developments is a key consideration when choosing an investment property. Infrastructure improvements, such as new transportation links, shopping centers, or business districts, can enhance property values over time. Investing in areas where significant infrastructure projects are planned or underway can lead to substantial capital growth as the neighbourhood develops and becomes more desirable.

4. Employment Opportunities

Investing in areas with strong employment opportunities can provide a stable rental income. Properties located near major employment hubs, business centers, or industrial zones are likely to attract tenants seeking convenience and proximity to their workplaces. An area's employment growth can be a strong indicator of its economic health and potential for property value appreciation.

Internal Outcomes: Evaluating the Property's Potential
1. Capital Growth

Capital growth refers to the increase in a property's value over time. When assessing potential investment properties, focus on those with strong historical performance in capital appreciation and positive future growth forecasts. Analyse market trends, historical sales data, and economic indicators to gauge a property's potential for value appreciation. Properties in emerging neighbourhoods or areas experiencing revitalization often present excellent capital growth opportunities.

2. Cashflow

Cashflow is the net income generated from a property after deducting all expenses. Positive cashflow properties generate more rental income than the cost of owning and managing them, providing a steady income stream. To ensure a property delivers positive cashflow, evaluate rental yields, ongoing expenses, and potential income. Properties in high-demand rental markets with competitive rental rates and low vacancy rates are ideal for generating strong cashflow.

3. Yield

Yield is the return on investment based on the property's value and rental income. It is expressed as a percentage and helps determine the profitability of an investment. Calculate both the gross yield (annual rental income divided by the property's purchase price) and the net yield (gross yield minus expenses). High-yield properties offer attractive returns and can be particularly beneficial for maximizing investment returns.

Crafting A Lucrative Portfolio

Once you've identified a good investment property, the next step is to build on this foundation to create a lucrative portfolio.

1. External Catalyst: The Perfect First Property

The initial step is to secure 'The Perfect Investment Property' as the cornerstone of your portfolio. This property should embody the qualities of a robust, growth-oriented investment, balancing affordability, lifestyle appeal, infrastructure proximity, and employment opportunities with strong capital growth, cashflow, and yield potential.

2. Internal Operations: Building and Leveraging Equity

- **Equity Growth:** As your property appreciates in value, you build equity. Equity is the difference between the property's market value and the amount you owe on your mortgage. Over time, as property values increase and you pay down your mortgage, your equity grows, enhancing your financial position.

- **Leveraging Equity:** With sufficient equity, you can leverage it to finance additional property purchases. By borrowing against your accumulated equity, you can invest in more properties without using additional personal funds. This strategy allows you to expand your portfolio and capitalize on further investment opportunities.

- **Repeat Purchases:** Use the equity from your first property to acquire additional 'perfect' properties. Each new purchase contributes to your growing portfolio, increasing your potential for capital growth, cashflow, and overall investment returns. Continually reinvest and build upon your initial successes to develop a diverse and profitable property portfolio.

Discovering the ideal investment property involves a careful assessment of external factors like affordability, lifestyle preferences, infrastructure developments, and employment opportunities, as well as internal outcomes such as capital growth, cashflow, and yield. By understanding these elements and applying strategic insights, you can identify properties with strong investment potential. Building a lucrative property portfolio requires not just finding the right investment but also effectively leveraging equity and making informed decisions to maximize returns. With a well-chosen initial property as your foundation, you can craft a successful investment strategy that offers financial growth and long-term prosperity.

Short-Term Accommodation and Tourism: High Rental Potential and Management Challenges

Investing in short-term accommodation, such as vacation rentals and tourism properties, can be an enticing opportunity for generating high rental income. With the rise of platforms like Airbnb, property owners have access to a global market of travellers seeking temporary lodging. However, while the potential for high rental returns is appealing, managing short-term rentals comes with its own set of challenges. This chapter explores both the lucrative aspects and the difficulties of investing in short-term accommodation, helping you make informed decisions in this dynamic sector.

The Potential for High Rentals

1. High Demand and Premium Rates

Short-term accommodation often commands higher rental rates compared to long-term leases. This is primarily due to the flexibility and convenience it offers travelers. Properties located in popular tourist destinations, near landmarks, or in vibrant urban areas can capitalize on high demand and premium pricing. For example, a well-located apartment in a city with a thriving tourism industry can attract nightly rates that significantly exceed those of traditional rental agreements.

2. Dynamic Pricing Strategies

One of the key advantages of short-term rentals is the ability to employ dynamic pricing strategies. Property owners can adjust rates based on factors such as seasonality, local events, and market demand. For instance, during peak tourist seasons or major local events, nightly rates can be increased to maximize income. Conversely, during off-peak periods, discounted rates can attract more guests and maintain occupancy.

3. Diverse Revenue Streams

Short-term rentals provide multiple revenue opportunities beyond just nightly stays. Additional income can be generated through premium services and amenities, such as airport transfers, guided tours, or special packages. By offering unique experiences or value-added services, property owners can enhance their rental income and differentiate their property from competitors.

4. Property Appreciation

Properties used for short-term rentals in high-demand areas can also benefit from appreciation in value. As the property becomes well-known and positively reviewed, its market value may increase. Additionally, well-maintained and popular short-term rental properties can attract higher offers if you decide to sell in the future.

Challenges of Managing Short-Term Rentals

1. Operational Demands

Managing short-term accommodations requires a high level of operational involvement. Unlike traditional rentals, short-term properties often need frequent cleaning, maintenance, and management of guest turnover. This can be time-consuming and may require hiring additional staff or outsourcing cleaning and maintenance services. Ensuring that the property is consistently guest-ready and well-maintained is crucial for positive reviews and repeat bookings.

2. Guest Expectations and Reviews

Guest expectations for short-term rentals can be quite high. Travelers often seek personalized experiences and expect high standards of cleanliness and comfort. Managing guest expectations and handling complaints effectively is essential to maintaining a good reputation and securing positive reviews. Negative reviews can significantly impact future bookings and rental income, making it important to address any issues promptly and professionally.

3. Regulatory and Legal Issues

Short-term rentals are subject to various local regulations and legal requirements, which can vary widely depending on the location. Some cities have strict rules regarding short-term rentals, including zoning restrictions, registration requirements, and limits on the number of rental days. Property owners must stay informed about local regulations and ensure compliance to avoid fines or legal complications.

4. Seasonality and Vacancy Risks

The income from short-term rentals can be highly seasonal, with peak periods offering high returns and off-peak periods potentially resulting in lower occupancy rates. Property owners must plan for fluctuations in rental income and budget for periods of lower demand. Effective marketing strategies and promotions can help mitigate vacancy risks, but they require ongoing effort and investment.

5. Increased Competition

The popularity of short-term rental platforms has led to increased competition. To stand out, property owners must invest in high-quality listings, professional photography, and compelling descriptions. Offering unique features, such as stylish decor, modern amenities, or exceptional customer service, can help attract and retain guests. Staying competitive requires ongoing effort to improve and differentiate your property from others in the market.

Strategies for Success

1. Optimize Your Listing

Create a detailed and attractive listing for your property. Invest in professional photography to showcase the property's best features and provide clear, accurate descriptions. Highlight unique aspects, such as stunning views, luxury amenities, or proximity to local attractions. A well-optimized listing can increase visibility and attract more bookings.

2. Invest in Quality and Comfort

Ensure that your property meets high standards of quality and comfort. Invest in comfortable furnishings, high-quality linens, and modern amenities. Pay attention to details such as cleanliness, maintenance, and guest convenience. A well-maintained and comfortable property enhances the guest experience and encourages positive reviews.

3. Leverage Technology

Utilize technology to streamline operations and enhance guest experiences. Property management software can help with booking management, guest communication, and scheduling cleaning services. Automated check-in and check-out processes can improve convenience for both guests and property owners.

4. Stay Informed and Compliant

Keep up-to-date with local regulations and industry trends. Regularly review and adjust your pricing strategies based on market conditions and seasonal trends. Monitor guest feedback and make improvements based on their suggestions. Staying informed and adaptable will help you navigate challenges and maximize rental income.

5. Build a Strong Brand

Develop a strong brand identity for your short-term rental property. Consistent branding, exceptional service, and a unique guest experience can set your property apart from competitors. Building a positive reputation and loyal guest base can lead to repeat bookings and word-of-mouth referrals.

Investing in short-term accommodation can offer substantial rental potential and lucrative returns, particularly in high-demand tourist destinations. However, managing short-term rentals comes with its own set of challenges, including operational demands, guest expectations, regulatory issues, and increased competition. By understanding these factors and implementing effective strategies, property owners can maximize their rental income and create a successful investment in the short-term rental market. Balancing the potential rewards with the associated responsibilities will help you achieve success in this dynamic and profitable sector.

What COVID-19 Taught Me About Investing in Property: The Need for Diversification

The COVID-19 pandemic fundamentally altered many aspects of our lives, including the property investment landscape. Before the pandemic, my investment strategy was straightforward: focus on high-return properties, particularly in the tourism sector. The idea was simple—invest in properties that catered to travellers and vacationers, capitalize on high nightly rates, and enjoy substantial rental income. However, the global crisis exposed the vulnerabilities of this approach and taught me valuable lessons about the importance of diversification in property investing.

The Allure of High-Return Properties

Before COVID-19, high-return properties, particularly those in the short-term rental or tourism sector, seemed like an ideal investment. These properties often offered premium rates, especially in popular tourist destinations. Platforms like Airbnb made it easier to reach a global audience, and the potential for substantial income was enticing. Investing in properties located near landmarks, beaches, or city centres promised high occupancy rates and impressive returns. The strategy was appealing for several reasons:
- Premium Rates: Short-term rentals typically commanded higher nightly rates compared to long-term leases.
- Flexibility: Dynamic pricing allowed for adjustments based on demand, events, and seasons.

- Diversified Income: Additional revenue could be generated through premium services and experiences offered to guests.

For a time, this approach seemed effective. Properties were consistently booked, and the rental income flowed smoothly. The high returns provided a sense of security and satisfaction.

The Impact of COVID-19

The onset of the COVID-19 pandemic threw the property market into turmoil. The tourism sector was among the hardest hit. Travel restrictions, lockdowns, and a general reluctance to engage in non-essential travel led to a dramatic decline in short-term rental bookings. My once-reliable high-return properties became a liability rather than an asset. The global crisis exposed several critical issues:

1. Travel Restrictions and Reduced Demand

With borders closing and people staying home, the demand for short-term rentals plummeted. My properties, once thriving on tourist traffic, experienced unprecedented vacancy rates. What had been a lucrative investment turned into a financial burden as the rental income dried up, and expenses continued to accumulate.

2. Financial Strain and Cash Flow Challenges

The drop in rental income highlighted the vulnerability of relying solely on one investment strategy. Properties that were once cash cows became sources of financial strain. The lack of diversification meant there was no safety net to cushion the impact of the pandemic's economic fallout. This period of financial uncertainty underscored the importance of having a diversified portfolio to manage risk.

3. Regulatory and Market Changes

The pandemic also brought about changes in regulations and market dynamics. Governments implemented new rules and restrictions for short-term rentals to curb the spread of the virus, and many local authorities imposed stricter regulations. The evolving regulatory environment further complicated the management and profitability of short-term rental properties.

The Lesson: The Need for Diversification

The COVID-19 experience taught me a crucial lesson about property investing: diversification is essential. Relying on a single strategy or type of property can expose investors to significant risks. Diversification helps spread risk and provides stability in the face of market fluctuations or unforeseen events. Here are the key takeaways from the pandemic:

1. Diversify Property Types

Investing in different types of properties—such as residential, commercial, and industrial—can help mitigate risks associated with market downturns in any one sector. While short-term rentals can offer high returns, diversifying into long-term rentals, commercial properties, or even real estate investment trusts (REITs) can provide a more balanced portfolio.

2. Explore Various Locations

Investing in properties across different locations can reduce the impact of regional market downturns or specific local issues. While a property in a popular tourist destination might have high potential returns, diversifying into areas with stable demand, such as residential neighborhoods or business districts, can provide a buffer against volatility.

3. Consider Different Income Streams

Diversification isn't just about varying property types or locations; it also involves exploring different income streams. For example, investing in properties that offer stable, long-term rental income can provide financial stability.

Additionally, incorporating income-generating strategies such as property development, renovation, or leasing commercial space can enhance overall returns.

4. Build a Cash Reserve

Maintaining a cash reserve is a prudent strategy to manage periods of reduced income or unexpected expenses. Having liquidity available can help cover mortgage payments, property maintenance, and other costs during times of economic uncertainty.

5. Stay Informed and Adaptable

The property market is constantly evolving, and staying informed about market trends, regulatory changes, and emerging investment opportunities is crucial. Being adaptable and willing to adjust your strategy in response to changing conditions can help mitigate risks and capitalize on new opportunities.

Moving Forward: A Revised Strategy

In response to the lessons learned during the pandemic, I have revised my investment strategy to incorporate diversification and adaptability. This revised approach includes:

- Investing in a Mix of Property Types: Incorporating a variety of property types into the portfolio to spread risk and enhance stability.
- Exploring Emerging Markets: Identifying and investing in emerging markets or up-and-coming areas with growth potential.
- Enhancing Property Management: Implementing strategies to improve property management and increase resilience against market fluctuations.
- Building Financial Resilience: Focusing on building financial reserves and maintaining flexibility to adapt to changing market conditions.

The COVID-19 pandemic was a challenging period that exposed the vulnerabilities of relying solely on high-return property investments in the tourism sector. However, it also provided invaluable lessons about the importance of diversification and adaptability in property investing. By incorporating a diverse range of property types, locations, and income streams, investors can better manage risks and create a more resilient portfolio. The experience has reshaped my approach to property investing, emphasizing the need for a balanced strategy that can withstand market fluctuations and economic uncertainties. As we move forward, these insights will guide more informed and strategic investment decisions, paving the way for sustained success in the dynamic world of property investing.

Chapter 3.5
INVEST IN PRIVATE EQUITY

Identifying Good Small Businesses for Private Equity Investment

Investing in private businesses can be a lucrative path to achieving substantial wealth. In this chapter, we will focus on identifying good small businesses for private equity investment, particularly those in Australia. According to the Australian Bureau of Statistics, a small business is defined as one that employs fewer than 20 people. However, for the purpose of private equity, we will expand this definition to include businesses with annual revenues starting from $500,000.

<u>Understanding the Characteristics of a Good Small Business</u>

Before diving into the specifics of small businesses, it is crucial to understand the general characteristics that make a business a worthy investment:

1. Stable and Growing Revenue: A good small business should demonstrate a track record of stable and growing revenue. Consistent revenue growth indicates a strong market position and effective management.

2. Profitability: Profitability is a key indicator of a business's health. A good small business should not only generate revenue but also convert a significant portion of it into profit.

3. Strong Cash Flow: Positive cash flow is essential for a business to sustain operations, reinvest in growth, and navigate financial challenges. Assessing cash flow statements provides insight into the business's liquidity and financial management.

4. Market Position and Competitive Advantage: Businesses with a unique selling proposition (USP) or competitive advantage in their market are more likely to succeed. This could be due to a unique product, exceptional service, strong brand, or operational efficiency.

5. Scalability: A good small business should have the potential for scalability. This means the business model can be expanded or replicated to increase revenue without a proportional increase in costs.

6. Management Team: The quality of the management team is often a decisive factor. Experienced, knowledgeable, and committed management can drive the business to new heights and effectively handle challenges.

7. Customer Base: A loyal and growing customer base is a positive sign. It indicates that the business is meeting customer needs and has potential for word-of-mouth growth.

8. Industry and Market Trends: Businesses operating in growing industries or markets are more likely to experience success. Understanding industry trends and market dynamics is crucial for evaluating the long-term potential of a business.

Evaluating Small Businesses with Annual Revenues Starting from $500,000

For private equity investment, small businesses with annual revenues starting from $500,000 can offer significant opportunities. Here are the steps and considerations for evaluating these businesses:

1. Financial Analysis:
 - Revenue and Profit Trends: analyse historical financial statements to assess revenue and profit trends. Look for consistent growth over the past three to five years.
 - Margin Analysis: Evaluate gross profit margins, operating margins, and net profit margins. Higher margins often indicate operational efficiency and pricing power.
 - Cash Flow Analysis: Examine cash flow statements to understand how the business generates and uses cash. Positive operating cash flow is a must.

2. Market Analysis:

- Market Size and Growth: Assess the size and growth potential of the market in which the business operates. Larger and growing markets offer more opportunities for expansion.

- Competitive Landscape: Identify key competitors and evaluate the business's competitive position. Look for businesses with a strong competitive advantage.

- Customer Demographics and Behaviour: Understand the customer base, including demographics, preferences, and buying behaviour. A business with a loyal and growing customer base is preferable.

3. Operational Analysis:

- Business Model: Evaluate the business model for scalability and sustainability. Consider how the business generates revenue, the cost structure, and potential for growth.

- Supply Chain and Operations: Assess the efficiency and reliability of the supply chain and operational processes. Strong operational management can enhance profitability and scalability.

- Technology and Innovation: Businesses that leverage technology and innovation to improve operations or offer unique products/services are often more competitive and scalable.

4. Management and Team Evaluation:

- Experience and Track Record: Assess the experience and track record of the management team. Successful past ventures and industry experience are positive indicators.

- Leadership and Vision: Evaluate the leadership qualities and strategic vision of the management. Strong leaders can inspire teams and drive the business forward.

- Team Dynamics and Culture: Consider the dynamics and culture within the team. A cohesive and motivated team can execute strategies effectively.

5. Legal and Regulatory Compliance:
   - Regulatory Environment: Understand the regulatory environment of the industry. Ensure the business complies with all relevant laws and regulations.
   - Intellectual Property: Evaluate the presence and protection of intellectual property, such as patents, trademarks, or proprietary technology.
   - Contracts and Agreements: Review key contracts and agreements with suppliers, customers, and employees. Ensure they are favourable and legally sound.

Examples of Good Small Businesses for Private Equity Investment

To illustrate, here are a few examples of small businesses with annual revenues starting from $500,000 that could be attractive for private equity investment:

   1. Tech Startups: Small tech companies offering innovative solutions or software-as-a-service (SaaS) platforms. These businesses often have high scalability potential and operate in growing markets.
   2. Niche Manufacturing Firms: Businesses that produce specialized products with a strong demand in niche markets. These firms can have high-profit margins and unique competitive advantages.
   3. Healthcare Services: Small healthcare providers, such as clinics or specialized service providers, often have stable revenue streams and growth potential due to increasing demand for healthcare services.
   4. E-commerce Businesses: Online retail businesses that have shown consistent revenue growth and have a strong brand presence. E-commerce continues to grow, offering significant opportunities for expansion.
   5. Professional Services Firms: Businesses offering specialized professional services, such as consulting, legal, or financial advisory services. These firms often have strong client relationships and recurring revenue.

Investing in small businesses through private equity can be a rewarding strategy, provided you identify businesses with strong fundamentals, growth potential, and effective management. By focusing on businesses with stable and growing revenue, profitability, strong cash flow, competitive advantages, scalability, and experienced management, you can increase the likelihood of a successful investment.

When evaluating small businesses with annual revenues starting from $500,000, thorough financial, market, operational, and management analysis is essential. By following a disciplined and comprehensive evaluation process, you can identify promising opportunities and make informed investment decisions.

As you proceed with your investment journey, remember that due diligence, patience, and a strategic approach are key to achieving long-term success in private equity investment.

Understanding Multiples in Private Business Valuation

When investing in private businesses, one of the most critical aspects is determining the value of the business. This chapter will focus on the concept of multiples, a commonly used method in business valuation. Understanding multiples and how to apply them correctly can significantly influence the success of your investments.

What Are Multiples?

Multiples are ratios used to compare a company's value to a particular financial metric, such as earnings, sales, or assets. They are widely used because they provide a quick and straightforward way to gauge the relative value of businesses. Common types of multiples include:

1. Price-to-Earnings (P/E) Ratio: This multiple compares the company's market value to its earnings. It is calculated by dividing the market price per share by the earnings per share (EPS).

2. Enterprise Value-to-EBITDA (EV/EBITDA): This ratio compares the enterprise value (EV) of a company to its earnings before interest, taxes, depreciation, and amortization (EBITDA). EV is the sum of a company's market capitalization, debt, and preferred shares, minus cash and cash equivalents.

3. Price-to-Sales (P/S) Ratio: This multiple compares the company's market value to its total sales or revenue. It is calculated by dividing the market capitalization by the total sales.

4. Price-to-Book (P/B) Ratio: This ratio compares a company's market value to its book value, calculated by dividing the market capitalization by the book value of equity.

5. Enterprise Value-to-Revenue (EV/Revenue): Similar to EV/EBITDA, this ratio compares the enterprise value to the total revenue of the company.

Why Use Multiples?

Multiples are useful for several reasons:

1. Simplicity: Multiples are easy to calculate and understand, making them accessible to investors without a deep financial background.

2. Comparability: They allow investors to compare companies of different sizes and industries by normalizing financial metrics.

3. Speed: Multiples provide a quick snapshot of valuation, which is particularly useful in competitive bidding situations.

4. Market Sentiment: They reflect market perceptions and expectations, offering insights into how other investors value similar businesses.

Applying Multiples to Private Business Valuation

When evaluating private businesses, it's essential to understand that these businesses often differ significantly from public companies. Private businesses might have less transparent financials, different growth prospects, and varied risk profiles. Therefore, adjusting multiples appropriately is crucial.

1. Earnings Multiples (P/E and EV/EBITDA):

- P/E Ratio: For private businesses, the P/E ratio can be insightful but should be used cautiously. Private companies may not have the same earnings consistency as public firms. When applying the P/E ratio, consider the company's historical earnings and adjust for any non-recurring items. Typically, a good P/E multiple for a stable private business might range from 5x to 15x, depending on the industry and growth prospects.

- EV/EBITDA: This is often more reliable for private companies as it accounts for debt and cash. A good EV/EBITDA multiple for private businesses usually ranges from 4x to 10x. Higher multiples might be justified for businesses with strong growth potential or unique competitive advantages.

2. Revenue Multiples (P/S and EV/Revenue):

- P/S Ratio: This can be useful for businesses with volatile or negative earnings. For private companies, a P/S multiple between 0.5x to 3x is generally considered reasonable. However, higher multiples might be warranted for businesses with high growth rates or strong brand equity.

- EV/Revenue: Similar to the P/S ratio but accounts for the company's capital structure. A good EV/Revenue multiple typically ranges from 1x to 4x, depending on the industry and business model.

3. Book Value Multiples (P/B Ratio):

- P/B Ratio: This is more relevant for asset-heavy businesses like manufacturing or real estate. For private companies, a P/B multiple ranging from 1x to 3x is common. Businesses with high returns on equity (ROE) might justify higher multiples.

Industry-Specific Multiples

Different industries have unique characteristics that affect their valuation multiples. Understanding these nuances is critical when assessing private businesses:

1. Technology: Tech companies, especially startups, often have high growth potential but might not be profitable. EV/Revenue and EV/EBITDA are commonly

used, with multiples ranging from 5x to 15x for revenue and 10x to 20x for EBITDA, reflecting high growth expectations.

2. Healthcare: This sector includes stable cash flow businesses like clinics and high-growth biotech firms. EV/EBITDA multiples typically range from 6x to 12x, while P/S multiples might range from 1x to 4x.

3. Retail: Retail businesses are often evaluated using P/S and EV/EBITDA multiples. P/S multiples might range from 0.5x to 2x, and EV/EBITDA from 4x to 8x, depending on factors like brand strength and online presence.

4. Manufacturing: Asset-heavy and often stable, manufacturing businesses are usually valued with EV/EBITDA and P/B ratios. EV/EBITDA multiples generally range from 5x to 8x, while P/B multiples can be from 1x to 3x.

Factors Influencing Multiples

Several factors can influence the appropriate multiples for a private business:

1. Growth Rate: Higher growth businesses typically command higher multiples. Assess the company's historical growth and future projections.

2. Profitability: More profitable businesses, with higher margins and consistent earnings, are usually valued higher.

3. Risk Profile: Higher risk (due to market, operational, or financial factors) typically leads to lower multiples. Evaluate the business's risk factors thoroughly.

4. Market Conditions: Economic and market conditions can affect multiples. During economic booms, multiples might be inflated, while downturns can depress them.

5. Competitive Position: Businesses with strong competitive advantages (e.g., patents, brand equity, market share) can justify higher multiples.

6. Management Quality: Experienced and capable management teams can enhance business value, leading to higher multiples.

Adjusting Multiples for Private Businesses

Private businesses often require adjustments to the multiples used for public companies:

1. Size and Scale: Smaller businesses generally face more risks and have less access to capital, warranting lower multiples.
2. Liquidity: Private businesses are less liquid than public ones, which can justify a discount to the multiples.
3. Control Premium: Acquiring a controlling interest in a private business might warrant a premium, reflecting the additional value of control.
4. Non-Recurring Items: Adjust earnings and other financial metrics for non-recurring items to get a clearer picture of sustainable performance.

Using multiples is a powerful and efficient method for valuing private businesses. By understanding the different types of multiples, their applications, and the factors influencing them, you can make more informed investment decisions. Remember to adjust multiples for the unique characteristics of private businesses and the specific industry context.

As you continue your journey in private equity investment, keep refining your approach to multiples, combining them with other valuation methods and thorough due diligence to identify the most promising opportunities.

Assessing Profitability in Small Businesses for Investment

Profitability is a cornerstone of business success and a key metric when evaluating potential investments. For private equity investors, understanding what constitutes a good profit in small businesses is crucial for making informed decisions. This chapter delves into the nuances of profitability, providing insights into what to look for when investing in small businesses.

Understanding Profitability Metrics

Before exploring what constitutes good profitability, it's important to understand the different metrics used to measure profit:

1. Gross Profit Margin: This metric shows the percentage of revenue that exceeds the cost of goods sold (COGS). It is calculated as:

Gross Profit Margin = (Revenue − COGS) x 100

A higher gross profit margin indicates that a business can effectively control its production costs.

2. Operating Profit Margin: Also known as EBIT (Earnings Before Interest and Taxes) margin, this metric measures the percentage of revenue remaining after all operating expenses are deducted. It is calculated as:

Operating Profit Margin = (Operating Profit / Revenue) x 100

This ratio indicates how well the business is managed and its operational efficiency.

3. Net Profit Margin: This metric measures the percentage of revenue that remains as profit after all expenses, including taxes and interest, are deducted. It is calculated as:

Net Profit Margin = (Net Profit / Revenue) x 100

The net profit margin provides a comprehensive view of the business's overall profitability.

4. Return on Assets (ROA): This metric shows how efficiently a business is using its assets to generate profit. It is calculated as:

ROA = (Net Profit / Total Assets) x 100

Higher ROA indicates efficient asset utilization.

5. Return on Equity (ROE): This metric measures the return generated on shareholders' equity. It is calculated as:

ROE = (Net Profit / Shareholders' Equity) x 100

A higher ROE indicates effective use of equity investments to generate profit.

<u>What Constitutes Good Profitability?</u>

Determining what constitutes good profitability depends on several factors, including industry standards, business model, and market conditions. Here are some general guidelines for assessing good profitability in small businesses:

1. Gross Profit Margin:
   - Benchmark: A good gross profit margin varies by industry but generally ranges from 20% to 50%. For example, retail businesses often have lower margins (around 20%-30%), while software companies can have higher margins (50% or more).
   - Analysis: Look for businesses with a gross profit margin above industry averages. This indicates effective cost management and pricing power.

2. Operating Profit Margin:
   - Benchmark: A healthy operating profit margin for small businesses typically ranges from 10% to 20%. Service-based businesses might have higher margins, while manufacturing businesses might have lower margins.
   - Analysis: Businesses with operating profit margins above 15% are generally considered well-managed and efficient. Look for consistent or improving operating margins over time.

3. Net Profit Margin:
   - Benchmark: Good net profit margins for small businesses generally range from 5% to 15%. Higher margins are preferable as they indicate better overall financial health.
   - Analysis: Consistent net profit margins above 10% are a positive sign. Pay attention to any significant fluctuations, which might indicate underlying issues.

4. Return on Assets (ROA):
   - Benchmark: A good ROA typically ranges from 5% to 10%. Higher ROA indicates efficient use of assets.
   - Analysis: Businesses with ROA above 7% are generally performing well. Compare ROA with industry averages to gauge efficiency.

5. Return on Equity (ROE):
 - Benchmark: A healthy ROE for small businesses ranges from 10% to 20%. Higher ROE indicates effective use of equity investments.
 - Analysis: Look for businesses with consistent ROE above 15%. High ROE, especially when combined with low debt levels, is a strong positive indicator.

Factors Influencing Profitability

Several factors influence the profitability of small businesses. Understanding these can help you assess whether a business's profit levels are sustainable and have potential for growth:

1. Industry Dynamics: Different industries have varying profitability norms. High-margin industries like software and pharmaceuticals generally offer better profit opportunities than low-margin industries like retail and manufacturing.

2. Cost Structure: Businesses with lower fixed and variable costs tend to have higher profit margins. Assess the business's cost control mechanisms and efficiency measures.

3. Pricing Power: Businesses that can set higher prices for their products or services without losing customers typically enjoy higher margins. Look for unique value propositions, strong brands, and less price-sensitive customer bases.

4. Scale and Efficiency: Larger businesses or those with economies of scale often have higher profitability due to lower per-unit costs. Assess the scalability of the business model and operational efficiency.

5. Management Quality: Effective management teams can significantly influence profitability through strategic decisions, cost control, and innovation. Evaluate the track record and expertise of the management team.

6. Market Conditions: Economic and market conditions impact profitability. Recessionary periods might reduce consumer spending, while boom periods can enhance sales and profits.

Assessing Profitability in Potential Investments

When evaluating potential investments, conducting thorough due diligence on profitability is essential. Here's a step-by-step approach:

1. Financial Statement Analysis:
   - Income Statement: Analyse revenue, COGS, operating expenses, and net profit. Look for trends and consistency in margins.
   - Balance Sheet: Assess assets, liabilities, and equity. Calculate ROA and ROE.
   - Cash Flow Statement: Evaluate operating cash flow, capital expenditures, and free cash flow. Positive and growing cash flow is a good sign.

2. Benchmarking:
   - Compare the business's profitability metrics with industry averages and key competitors. This helps contextualize the business's performance.

3. Trend Analysis:
   - Examine historical profitability trends. Consistent or improving margins indicate a stable or growing business.

4. Ratio Analysis:
   - Calculate and analyse key ratios like gross profit margin, operating profit margin, net profit margin, ROA, and ROE. Look for ratios above industry norms.

5. Qualitative Factors:
   - Evaluate qualitative factors such as management quality, competitive position, market conditions, and business model. These factors influence future profitability.

Examples of Good Profitability in Small Businesses

To illustrate, here are a few examples of small businesses with good profitability:

1. Software-as-a-Service (SaaS) Company:
   - Gross Profit Margin: 70%
   - Operating Profit Margin: 25%
   - Net Profit Margin: 20%

- ROA: 15%
   - ROE: 25%
   - Analysis: High margins and returns indicate strong pricing power, efficient operations, and effective management.

2. Healthcare Clinic:
   - Gross Profit Margin: 50%
   - Operating Profit Margin: 18%
   - Net Profit Margin: 12%
   - ROA: 10%
   - ROE: 18%
   - Analysis: Good profitability metrics reflect stable demand, effective cost control, and solid management.

3. E-commerce Business:
   - Gross Profit Margin: 40%
   - Operating Profit Margin: 15%
   - Net Profit Margin: 10%
   - ROA: 8%
   - ROE: 15%
   - Analysis: Healthy margins indicate strong online presence, operational efficiency, and growth potential.

Profitability is a key determinant of a business's health and a crucial factor in investment decisions. By understanding and analysing various profitability metrics—gross profit margin, operating profit margin, net profit margin, ROA, and ROE—you can assess the financial health and potential of small businesses.

Good profitability varies by industry and is influenced by factors such as cost structure, pricing power, scalability, and management quality. Conduct thorough due diligence, compare against industry benchmarks, and consider qualitative factors to make informed investment decisions.

As you navigate the world of private equity investment, remember that profitability is not just about current performance but also about sustainability and growth potential. With careful analysis and strategic insights, you can identify and invest in small businesses with robust profitability and promising futures.

Key Industries for Small Businesses

Small businesses form the backbone of many economies, including Australia. They span a diverse range of industries, each with unique opportunities and challenges. This chapter explores the main industries where small businesses thrive, providing a breakdown of these sectors and highlighting the primary types of businesses within each.

Overview of Small Business Industries
Small businesses are prevalent in several key industries, including:
1. Retail Trade
2. Professional, Scientific, and Technical Services
3. Construction
4. Healthcare and Social Assistance
5. Accommodation and Food Services
6. Arts and Recreation Services
7. Education and Training
8. Manufacturing
9. Wholesale Trade
10. Administrative and Support Services
11. Information Media and Telecommunications

Each of these industries has a significant presence of small businesses, contributing to economic growth and employment. Let's delve into each sector to understand the types of small businesses that dominate these industries.

1. Retail Trade

Retail trade is a major sector for small businesses, encompassing a variety of establishments that sell goods directly to consumers.

Types of Small Businesses:
- Specialty Stores: These include boutiques, gift shops, and stores selling niche products such as books, toys, or electronics.
- Grocery Stores: Small, independent grocery stores and convenience stores.
- Online Retailers: E-commerce businesses selling products through online platforms.

Industry Characteristics:
- High competition
- Emphasis on customer service and location
- Increasing importance of online presence and digital marketing

2. Professional, Scientific, and Technical Services

This industry includes a wide range of professional services that require specialized knowledge and expertise.

Types of Small Businesses:
- Legal Services: Small law firms and independent lawyers.
- Accounting Services: Independent accountants and small accounting firms.
- Consulting: Management consultants, IT consultants, and marketing consultants.
- Architectural and Engineering Services: Small architectural firms and engineering consultancies.

Industry Characteristics:
- High reliance on skilled labour
- Emphasis on professional credentials and experience
- Importance of reputation and client relationships

3. Construction

The construction industry has a significant number of small businesses involved in building and infrastructure projects.

Types of Small Businesses:
- General Contractors: Small firms managing construction projects.
- Specialty Trade Contractors: Businesses specializing in plumbing, electrical work, painting, and carpentry.
- Home Builders: Small companies focused on residential construction.

Industry Characteristics:
- Cyclical nature tied to economic conditions
- High capital requirements for equipment and materials
- Importance of regulatory compliance and safety standards

4. Healthcare and Social Assistance

This sector includes a variety of services aimed at improving health and well-being.

Types of Small Businesses:
- Medical Practices: Independent doctors, dentists, and other healthcare practitioners.
- Allied Health Services: Physiotherapists, chiropractors, and occupational therapists.
- Childcare Services: Daycare centres and preschools.
- Aged Care Services: Small nursing homes and home care services.

Industry Characteristics:
- Steady demand driven by population demographics
- Regulatory requirements and standards
- High initial setup costs for medical equipment and facilities

5. Accommodation and Food Services

The hospitality industry has a large number of small businesses providing lodging and dining services.

Types of Small Businesses:
- Restaurants and Cafes: Independent eateries and coffee shops.
- Bed and Breakfasts: Small, family-run lodging establishments.

- **Catering Services**: Businesses providing food for events and functions.

Industry Characteristics:
- High competition and turnover
- Importance of customer experience and service quality
- Seasonal variations in demand

6. Arts and Recreation Services

This industry encompasses businesses providing cultural, recreational, and entertainment services.

Types of Small Businesses:
- Fitness Centres: Gyms and personal training studios.
- Creative Arts: Art galleries, dance studios, and music schools.
- Tourism Services: Small tour operators and travel agencies.

Industry Characteristics:
- Highly dependent on discretionary spending
- Seasonal and economic fluctuations affecting demand
- Creative and innovative business models

7. Education and Training

The education sector includes a range of small businesses focused on learning and development.

Types of Small Businesses:
- Tutoring Services: Independent tutors and tutoring centers.
- Vocational Training: Trade schools and training providers.
- Language Schools: Institutions offering language instruction.

Industry Characteristics:
- Increasing demand for lifelong learning and skills development
- Regulatory and accreditation requirements
- Importance of reputation and quality of instruction

8. Manufacturing

Although traditionally associated with larger firms, the manufacturing sector includes many small businesses producing a variety of goods.

Types of Small Businesses:
- Artisanal Producers: Small-scale producers of handmade goods, such as crafts and food products.
- Niche Manufacturers: Businesses producing specialized industrial components or consumer products.
- Custom Manufacturing: Companies offering custom fabrication and production services.

Industry Characteristics:
- Capital-intensive with high initial investment costs
- Emphasis on innovation and quality control
- Competitive pressure from larger manufacturers

9. Wholesale Trade

This sector includes businesses that sell goods in large quantities to retailers or other businesses.

Types of Small Businesses:
- Distributors: Companies distributing products from manufacturers to retailers.
- Import/Export Firms: Businesses specializing in importing and exporting goods.
- Specialty Wholesalers: Wholesalers focusing on specific product categories.

Industry Characteristics:
- Requires strong supply chain management
- Emphasis on logistics and inventory control
- Competitive pricing and volume sales strategies

10. Administrative and Support Services

This industry includes businesses providing support services to other businesses.

Types of Small Businesses:
- Cleaning Services: Commercial and residential cleaning companies.
- Employment Services: Staffing agencies and recruitment firms.
- Security Services: Private security companies and consulting firms.

Industry Characteristics:
- Steady demand for outsourced services
- Emphasis on reliability and service quality
- Competitive market with low barriers to entry

11. Information Media and Telecommunications

This sector covers businesses involved in media production and telecommunications services.

Types of Small Businesses:
- Digital Media: Content creators, social media managers, and online publishers.
- IT Services: Small firms offering IT support, web development, and cybersecurity services.
- Telecommunications Resellers: Companies reselling telecom services.

Industry Characteristics:
- Rapid technological change and innovation
- High competition in digital media and IT services
- Importance of technical expertise and customer service

Small businesses are integral to a diverse range of industries, each offering unique opportunities for investment and growth. By understanding the characteristics and dominant types of small businesses within each industry, investors can make informed decisions and identify promising opportunities.

Whether it's a boutique retail store, a healthcare practice, a construction firm, or a digital media company, small businesses drive innovation, employment, and economic development. As you explore potential investments, consider the industry dynamics, business models, and profitability metrics to identify the most promising small business opportunities.

Investing in Small Businesses – Lessons from COVID-19

The COVID-19 pandemic was a profound global event that reshaped economies, societies, and industries. As an investor in small businesses, the pandemic provided critical insights into the resilience and necessity of various types of businesses. Some sectors faced severe disruptions, while others proved to be indispensable. This chapter delves into the lessons learned from the pandemic, emphasizing the importance of investing in essential services versus discretionary ones.

The Impact of COVID-19 on Small Businesses

The pandemic highlighted the stark contrast between businesses that are essential and those that are not. Lockdowns, social distancing measures, and economic uncertainties affected small businesses across the board, but the degree of impact varied significantly.

Severely Impacted Sectors:
- Hospitality: Restaurants, bars, and cafes faced prolonged closures, reduced customer capacity, and shifting consumer behavior.
- Retail (Non-Essential): Clothing stores, bookshops, and other non-essential retailers struggled with reduced foot traffic and increased online competition.
- Entertainment and Leisure: Gyms, theaters, and event venues experienced significant declines as people stayed home.

Resilient or Thriving Sectors:
- Healthcare: General practitioners, pharmacies, and healthcare services remained critical, often experiencing increased demand.
- Legal and Financial Services: Solicitors, accountants, and financial advisors continued to be essential, providing services that individuals and businesses could not do without.

- Grocery and Convenience Stores: These businesses saw increased patronage as people prioritized basic necessities.

Lessons Learned from Investing During the Pandemic

The pandemic underscored several key principles for investing in small businesses:

1. Essential vs. Non-Essential Services

   - Essential Services: These are businesses that people rely on regardless of economic conditions. Healthcare providers, legal services, grocery stores, and utility providers are examples of businesses that saw sustained demand during the pandemic. Investing in such sectors can provide a safety net during economic downturns.

   - Non-Essential Services: Businesses in hospitality, leisure, and luxury goods often face significant volatility during crises. While they can be highly profitable in stable times, they pose higher risks during unforeseen disruptions.

2. Business Model Flexibility

   - Adaptability: Businesses that could pivot quickly to new models fared better. For example, restaurants that switched to takeout and delivery services managed to sustain revenue. The ability to adapt to changing circumstances is a valuable trait in any business.

   - Digital Transformation: Companies that embraced e-commerce, online services, and remote work adapted more smoothly. The pandemic accelerated digital transformation, making it a critical factor for future resilience.

3. Financial Health and Reserves

   - Liquidity: Businesses with strong cash reserves and low debt levels were better positioned to weather the storm. Ensuring liquidity is essential for surviving periods of reduced revenue.

   - Cost Management: Efficient cost management and the ability to reduce expenses quickly without compromising core operations helped businesses stay afloat.

4. Customer Relationships and Loyalty

- Trust and Loyalty: Businesses with strong customer relationships and loyalty programs maintained patronage even during tough times. Building a loyal customer base can provide a buffer against economic shocks.

- Communication: Transparent and regular communication with customers about safety measures, operational changes, and service availability fostered trust and continued engagement.

Case Study: The Licensed Bar and Coffee Shop

Reflecting on a specific investment—a licensed bar that operated as a coffee shop during the day and a bar in the evening—provides a practical example of these lessons.

Impact of COVID-19:
- Initial Disruption: The bar and coffee shop faced immediate challenges with lockdowns, reduced operating hours, and social distancing requirements. Customer traffic plummeted, and revenue streams were severely affected.
- Adaptation Attempts: Attempts to pivot included offering takeaway coffee and packaged meals, but these efforts could not fully compensate for the loss of in-house patronage, especially during evenings when the bar typically generated higher revenue.

Key Takeaways:
- Non-Essential Nature: The bar and coffee shop, while popular in normal times, proved to be non-essential during the pandemic. People prioritized health, groceries, and essential services over social and recreational activities.
- Vulnerability to Disruptions: Hospitality businesses are highly susceptible to disruptions that limit physical gatherings. The reliance on in-person customer experiences made it difficult to sustain operations during lockdowns.

- Future Considerations: For future investments, focusing on sectors that provide essential services or have adaptable business models is crucial. Diversifying investments to include essential services can balance the portfolio and reduce risk.

<u>Investing in Essential Services</u>
Based on the lessons from COVID-19, investing in businesses that provide essential services offers a more stable and resilient option. Here are some sectors and types of small businesses to consider:

1. Healthcare and Wellness
   - General Practitioners: Consistently in demand for routine and emergency healthcare.
   - Pharmacies: Essential for medication and health products.
   - Mental Health Services: Increasing awareness and acceptance of mental health care make this a growing field.

2. Legal and Financial Services
   - Solicitors: Necessary for legal advice, documentation, and litigation.
   - Accountants and Tax Advisors: Essential for financial management, especially during economic upheavals.
   - Financial Planners: Increasingly important for personal and business financial stability.

3. Food and Grocery Retail
   - Grocery Stores: Always in demand for basic necessities.
   - Specialty Food Shops: Health food stores and organic markets cater to niche but essential consumer needs.

4. Utilities and Infrastructure
   - Utility Services: Providers of electricity, water, and internet are indispensable.
   - Maintenance and Repair Services: Plumbing, electrical, and general home repair services remain necessary regardless of economic conditions.

The COVID-19 pandemic was a powerful reminder of the importance of investing in businesses that offer essential services. While non-essential businesses can thrive in stable times, their vulnerability during crises makes them riskier investments. By focusing on sectors that provide indispensable services, investors can build more resilient portfolios capable of weathering economic uncertainties.

As you evaluate potential investments, consider the lessons from the pandemic. Prioritize businesses that demonstrate adaptability, financial health, and essential service offerings. By doing so, you can position yourself for long-term success and stability, even in the face of future disruptions.

Identifying Good Entry Points for Small Private Business Investments

Investing in small private businesses can be a rewarding venture, especially when you identify opportunities with strong potential for growth and stability. One key to success is finding the right entry points—businesses that are not only essential but also available at attractive valuations. This chapter will explore what makes a good entry point for small private business investments, focusing on essential services, favourable purchase multiples, and high returns.

Characteristics of a Good Entry Point

A good entry point for a small private business investment typically has the following characteristics:

1. Essential Services: The business operates in an industry that provides essential services, ensuring steady demand even during economic downturns.

2. Favourable Purchase Multiples: The business is available at a lower multiple of its earnings or revenue, making it a cost-effective investment with potential for high returns.

3. Solid Financials: The business has a stable revenue stream, healthy profit margins, and manageable debt levels.

4. **Growth Potential:** There is room for expansion, whether through increasing market share, expanding services, or improving operational efficiency.

5. **Strong Customer Base:** A loyal and growing customer base ensures consistent revenue.

Example: Hairdressing Salon

Business Overview:
- Revenue: $500,000
- Profit: $100,000
- Purchase Price: $100,000 (1x profit)

Why It's a Good Entry Point:
- Essential Service: Hairdressing is a basic personal care service with consistent demand.
- Low Multiple: Purchasing at 1x profit is a favourable multiple, offering a high return on investment.
- Growth Potential: Opportunities to expand services, increase prices, or open additional locations.
- Customer Loyalty: Hair salons often have a loyal customer base who return regularly for services.

Example: Small Accounting Firm

Business Overview:
- Revenue: $600,000
- Profit: $120,000
- Purchase Price: $150,000 (1.25x profit)

Why It's a Good Entry Point:
- Essential Service: Accounting services are necessary for individuals and businesses, ensuring steady demand.
- Moderate Multiple: The purchase price of 1.25x profit is still reasonable, with good potential for return.

- Growth Potential: Opportunities to expand client base, offer additional financial services, or specialize in lucrative niches like tax planning.
- Recession-Proof: Demand for accounting services remains stable during economic downturns as businesses and individuals still need financial management.

Example: Veterinary Clinic

Business Overview:
- Revenue: $700,000
- Profit: $140,000
- Purchase Price: $210,000 (1.5x profit)

Why It's a Good Entry Point:
- Essential Service: Veterinary services are critical for pet owners, ensuring consistent demand.
- Reasonable Multiple: Purchasing at 1.5x profit offers a balance between affordability and potential return.
- Growth Potential: Opportunities to expand services (e.g., grooming, boarding), increase marketing efforts, or open additional clinics.
- Customer Loyalty: Pet owners are often loyal to their veterinarians, ensuring repeat business.

Example: Small Pharmacy

Business Overview:
- Revenue: $800,000
- Profit: $160,000
- Purchase Price: $240,000 (1.5x profit)

Why It's a Good Entry Point:
- Essential Service: Pharmacies provide critical healthcare products and services.
- Reasonable Multiple: 1.5x profit is a reasonable multiple with strong return potential.

- Growth Potential: Expanding product lines, offering additional health services, or enhancing online sales can drive growth.
- Steady Demand: Healthcare needs are constant, making pharmacies recession-proof.

Example: Childcare Center

Business Overview:
- Revenue: $900,000
- Profit: $180,000
- Purchase Price: $270,000 (1.5x profit)

Why It's a Good Entry Point:
- Essential Service: Childcare services are essential for working families, ensuring steady demand.
- Reasonable Multiple: 1.5x profit offers good value and return potential.
- Growth Potential: Opportunities to expand capacity, offer additional educational programs, or open new centres.
- Customer Loyalty: Parents often remain loyal to childcare providers, ensuring repeat business.

Example: Home Healthcare Services

Business Overview:
- Revenue: $1,000,000
- Profit: $200,000
- Purchase Price: $300,000 (1.5x profit)

Why It's a Good Entry Point:
- Essential Service: Home healthcare is critical for elderly and disabled individuals.
- Reasonable Multiple: 1.5x profit is an attractive valuation for an essential service with high demand.
- Growth Potential: Opportunities to expand services, increase client base, or specialize in niche markets like post-surgical care.

- Steady Demand: An aging population ensures growing demand for home healthcare services.

Key Considerations for Investors

When evaluating small private businesses for investment, consider the following:

1. Due Diligence: Thoroughly investigate the business's financials, operations, and market position. Ensure that the revenue and profit figures are accurate and sustainable.
2. Industry Trends: Understand the broader industry trends and potential challenges. Essential services often benefit from stable or growing demand.
3. Management Team: Assess the competence and experience of the current management team. Strong leadership can significantly impact business performance.
4. Competitive Landscape: Analyse the competition and the business's unique value proposition. A strong competitive edge can drive long-term success.
5. **Exit Strategy**: Plan your exit strategy in advance. Consider how you will realize your returns, whether through selling the business, merging with another entity, or other means.

Identifying good entry points for small private business investments requires careful consideration of the business's essential nature, favourable purchase multiples, solid financials, growth potential, and customer loyalty. By focusing on essential services and securing businesses at reasonable valuations, investors can achieve high returns and build a resilient investment portfolio.

The examples provided—hairdressing salons, accounting firms, veterinary clinics, pharmacies, childcare centres, and home healthcare services—illustrate the types of businesses that can offer attractive entry points. These businesses provide essential services with consistent demand, making them stable and potentially profitable investments. As you explore investment opportunities, prioritize businesses that align with these criteria to maximize your chances of success.

Chapter 3.6
The Power of Leverage and the Art of the Buyout

In the world of investing, few strategies have proven to be as potent and profitable as leveraging buyouts. This approach, particularly when applied to property and private businesses, stands as one of the most effective methods for wealth accumulation. The essence of leveraging buyouts lies in the ability to use borrowed capital to amplify returns on investments, and when executed with precision, it can transform ordinary investments into extraordinary gains.

The Leverage Advantage

Leverage is the force multiplier in investing, allowing you to control a more substantial asset with a relatively small amount of your own capital. This principle is at the core of leveraged buyouts (LBOs), where investors use a combination of equity and debt to acquire assets, whether they be properties or businesses. The power of leverage comes from its capacity to magnify returns, allowing investors to achieve higher profit margins than would be possible with equity alone.

In property investing, leverage enables you to control high-value assets with a fraction of the total cost. For instance, with a 20% down payment, you can purchase a property worth five times your investment. If the property appreciates or generates rental income, your returns are based on the entire value of the property, not just your initial investment. This amplification of returns is where the true power of leverage shines, making property a lucrative option for those who understand and can manage the associated risks.

Private business investing, similarly, benefits from leverage. By acquiring businesses at favourable prices and using debt to fund a significant portion of the purchase, investors can significantly increase their potential returns. This approach requires a careful analysis of the target business's value, potential for growth, and the terms of the financing. When done correctly, leveraging allows investors to control a substantial business with relatively little capital, reaping the rewards of its growth and profitability.

The Art of Buying Businesses at Good Prices

Successful leveraged buyouts depend not only on the effective use of leverage but also on acquiring businesses or properties at advantageous prices. The key is to identify undervalued assets that possess significant growth potential. This involves thorough research, valuation analysis, and negotiation skills. The goal is to acquire assets at prices that allow for substantial upside while managing the risks associated with leverage.

In private business investing, this means finding companies that are undervalued or underperforming but have the potential for improvement. Investors look for businesses with strong fundamentals, a solid market position, and the potential for operational improvements. By acquiring these businesses at lower multiples and implementing strategic changes, investors can enhance their value, generate higher returns, and create wealth over time.

Stephen Schwarzman and Blackstone: A Case Study

A prime example of leveraging buyouts to build immense wealth is Stephen Schwarzman and his firm, Blackstone. In his book, *What It Takes*, Schwarzman recounts the journey of creating one of the world's most powerful investment companies. Blackstone's success is rooted in its expertise in leveraged buyouts, where it has employed a strategic combination of leverage, capital, and management skills to acquire and transform businesses.

Schwarzman's approach to investing emphasizes the importance of identifying value and deploying leverage effectively. By acquiring businesses and properties at advantageous prices, and then applying operational improvements and strategic management, Blackstone has been able to achieve exceptional returns on its investments. Schwarzman's story illustrates the remarkable potential of leveraging buyouts when executed with skill and precision.

The Path to Wealth

For investors looking to build significant wealth, leveraging buyouts in property and private business investments offers a powerful path. The combination of using borrowed funds to amplify returns and acquiring undervalued assets positions investors for substantial gains. However, this strategy requires a deep understanding of the market, meticulous planning, and a readiness to manage the risks associated with leverage.

Investing in property allows individuals to control valuable assets with minimal initial capital, while private business investing enables investors to acquire and enhance companies, benefiting from their growth and profitability. Both approaches leverage the principle of magnifying returns through debt, making them highly effective tools for wealth creation.

In conclusion, leveraging buyouts stand as one of the most compelling strategies in the investment world. By applying leverage in property and private business investments, and by acquiring assets at favourable prices, investors can achieve extraordinary returns and build substantial wealth. The success stories of figures like Stephen Schwarzman and firms like Blackstone underscore the potential of this approach. For those willing to embrace the challenges and opportunities of leveraged investing, the rewards can be transformative.

As you embark on your journey to financial success, remember the power of leverage and the art of buying assets at the right price. With careful planning, strategic execution, and a keen eye for value, leveraging buyouts can be the key to unlocking exceptional wealth and achieving your investment goals.

PART 4.
GROUP INVESTING

Chapter 4.1
THE POWER OF GROUP INVESTING:
Pooling Resources to Achieve Greater Wealth

Investing as a group can be a powerful strategy for growing wealth more quickly than going it alone. By pooling funds and sharing investment ideas, a group of like-minded individuals can achieve significant financial milestones faster and more efficiently. This approach mirrors the strategies of large investment funds, but it can be effectively applied to private investing among friends and family. In this chapter, we'll explore the benefits of group investing, the importance of shared ideas, and the potential challenges that can arise.

The Concept of Group Investing

Group investing involves multiple individuals coming together to pool their financial resources and invest collectively. This method allows participants to leverage each other's knowledge, spread risk, and access larger investment opportunities that might be out of reach individually.
Key Elements of Group Investing:
- Pooling Funds: Combining financial resources to create a larger investment pool.
- Shared Ideas: Collaboratively identifying and evaluating investment opportunities.
- Diversification: Spreading investments across different assets to reduce risk.
- Collective Decision-Making: Making investment decisions as a group, based on consensus or voting.

Benefits of Group Investing

1. Increased Capital: By pooling funds, the group can access more substantial investment opportunities, which can lead to higher returns.
2. Diversification: Group investing allows for a broader range of investments, reducing the overall risk by not putting all eggs in one basket.
3. Shared Expertise: Each member brings unique knowledge and skills, enhancing the group's ability to make informed decisions.
4. Risk Mitigation: Sharing the financial risk among several investors lessens the burden on any single individual.
5. Networking and Support: Group investing fosters a supportive environment where members can learn from each other and share successes and challenges.

Setting Up a Group Investment

To successfully set up a group investment, several key steps need to be followed:

1. Forming the Group:
   - Identify Potential Members: Look for individuals who share similar financial goals, investment philosophies, and levels of commitment.
   - Define Roles and Responsibilities: Establish clear roles for each member, such as decision-makers, researchers, and financial managers.

2. Establishing a Structure:
   - Legal Structure: Choose an appropriate legal structure, such as a partnership, limited liability company (LLC), or investment club, to formalize the group.
   - Operating Agreement: Draft an agreement outlining the rules, decision-making processes, profit-sharing arrangements, and dispute resolution methods.

3. Pooling Funds:
   - Initial Contributions: Determine the amount each member will contribute initially and any ongoing contributions.
   - Bank Account: Open a dedicated bank account for the group's investments to ensure transparency and proper fund management.

4. Decision-Making Process:
   - Voting System: Establish a voting system or consensus-based approach for making investment decisions.
   - Regular Meetings: Schedule regular meetings to discuss potential investments, review portfolio performance, and address any issues.

Finding and Evaluating Investment Opportunities

One of the most critical aspects of group investing is identifying and evaluating potential investment opportunities. This process requires collective input and a thorough analysis to ensure the chosen investments align with the group's goals.

1. Research and Analysis:
   - Market Research: Conduct comprehensive market research to identify promising investment opportunities.
   - Due Diligence: Perform detailed due diligence on each potential investment, including financial analysis, market trends, and risk assessment.
   - Expert Consultation: Seek advice from financial experts or consultants if needed to gain additional insights.

2. Criteria for Investment:
   - Alignment with Goals: Ensure the investment aligns with the group's financial goals and risk tolerance.

- Potential for Growth: Assess the potential for capital appreciation and income generation.

- Risk vs. Reward: Evaluate the risk-reward ratio to determine if the potential returns justify the risks involved.

3. Decision-Making:

- Presentation: Members can present their research and recommendations to the group.

- Discussion and Debate: Engage in open discussions to evaluate the pros and cons of each investment opportunity.

- Final Decision: Use the established voting system or consensus method to make the final investment decision.

Examples of Group Investments

To illustrate the power of group investing, consider the following examples of potential investment opportunities:

1. Real Estate:

- Residential Property: Pooling funds to purchase rental properties can generate consistent rental income and potential capital appreciation.

- Commercial Property: Investing in commercial real estate, such as office buildings or retail spaces, can provide higher returns but with increased risk.

2. Small Businesses:

- Local Startups: Investing in local startups or small businesses with high growth potential can yield significant returns if the business succeeds.

- Franchises: Purchasing a franchise can offer a proven business model with support from the franchisor, reducing some of the risks associated with startups.

3. Stock Market:

- Mutual Funds: Investing in mutual funds allows the group to diversify across a wide range of stocks and bonds, managed by professional fund managers.

- Individual Stocks: Selecting and investing in individual stocks can offer higher returns but requires careful research and monitoring.

Overcoming Challenges in Group Investing

While group investing has many benefits, it also comes with potential challenges that need to be addressed to ensure success.

1. Ego and Personal Agendas:
   - Open Communication: Foster a culture of open and honest communication where members feel comfortable sharing their ideas and concerns.
   - Objective Decision-Making: Encourage members to focus on objective criteria rather than personal biases when evaluating investments.

2. Disagreements and Conflicts:
   - Conflict Resolution Mechanisms: Establish clear conflict resolution mechanisms in the operating agreement to address disputes constructively.
   - Mediation: Consider involving a neutral third party, such as a financial advisor or mediator, to help resolve conflicts if necessary.

3. Commitment and Participation:
   - Clear Expectations: Set clear expectations for each member's participation and contribution to the group.
   - Regular Updates: Provide regular updates on the group's investments and financial performance to keep all members informed and engaged.

4. Management and Administration:
   - Professional Management: If the group's investments become too complex to manage internally, consider hiring professional management or administrative support.
   - Record Keeping: Maintain accurate and transparent records of all transactions, decisions, and communications to ensure accountability and transparency.

The Importance of Shared Ideas

For group investing to be successful, it is crucial that all members share the same investment philosophy and goals. Differences in investment strategies and risk tolerance can lead to conflicts and undermine the group's effectiveness.

1. Alignment of Goals:
   - Common Objectives: Ensure that all members have common financial objectives, such as long-term growth, income generation, or capital preservation.
   - Risk Tolerance: Align the group's risk tolerance to avoid disagreements over investment decisions.

2. Collaborative Mindset:
   - Teamwork: Foster a collaborative mindset where members work together towards common goals rather than pursuing individual agendas.
   - Respect for Expertise: Recognize and respect the expertise and opinions of each member, leveraging their strengths to make better-informed decisions.

3. Education and Training:
   - Continuous Learning: Encourage continuous learning and education to keep all members informed about market trends, investment strategies, and financial management.
   - Workshops and Seminars: Organize workshops and seminars to enhance the group's collective knowledge and skills.

Group investing offers a powerful way to grow wealth more quickly by pooling resources and sharing investment ideas. By working together, a group of like-minded individuals can access larger investment opportunities, spread risk, and benefit from shared expertise. However, for group investing to be successful, it is crucial to establish a strong foundation with clear roles, transparent communication, and aligned goals.

The key to success lies in finding a group of individuals who share the same investment philosophy and are committed to working together towards common financial objectives. By fostering a collaborative mindset, overcoming potential challenges, and continuously learning and adapting, group investing can be a highly rewarding and effective strategy for achieving financial milestones.

In summary, whether it's investing in real estate, small businesses, or the stock market, group investing allows for greater financial leverage, diversification, and support. By pooling resources and sharing ideas, you can achieve big milestones more quickly and enjoy the benefits of collective success.

Chapter 4.2
FAMILY-DRIVEN INVESTING;
Building on a Legacy and Creating Wealth Together

Starting your investment journey with your family can be a powerful way to build wealth and secure financial stability for future generations. Imagine if your parents already have an investment portfolio, and you have the opportunity to continue building on it. This chapter explores the benefits of family-driven investing, how to maximize the advantages of a shared family portfolio, and why having individual jobs while sharing expenses can significantly boost your family's financial growth.

The Power of a Family Portfolio

When you start with an existing family portfolio, you have a strong foundation to build upon. This approach leverages the previous generation's financial wisdom, investments, and accumulated wealth, creating a cumulative effect that can accelerate growth.

Advantages of a Family Portfolio:
- Legacy Building: Continue the financial legacy created by previous generations, ensuring that wealth is preserved and grown over time.
- Shared Knowledge: Benefit from the investment knowledge and experience of family members, enhancing decision-making.
- Compounded Growth: Investments made by previous generations have had time to mature, providing a robust starting point for further growth.
- Risk Mitigation: Diversified investments in the family portfolio can reduce individual risk and provide financial security.

The Challenge of Family Businesses

Many families start small businesses with the intention of involving the whole family. While this can be rewarding, it often poses significant challenges. Small businesses may not generate enough income to support all family members, leading to financial strain and limited growth opportunities.

Common Challenges:

- Limited Income: A small business may not provide sufficient income to support the entire family.
- Overdependence: Relying solely on the business for income can be risky, especially during economic downturns.
- Conflict: Family dynamics can lead to conflicts over business decisions, impacting both the business and family relationships.
- Growth Constraints: Limited resources and market reach can hinder the business's growth potential.

A Different Approach: Individual Jobs and Shared Investments

Instead of all family members working in a small business, consider a different approach where each person has their own job, contributing to the household income while sharing expenses. This strategy allows the family to save more and invest collectively as passive investors.

Benefits of This Approach:
- Stable Income: Individual jobs provide a stable income stream, reducing financial dependence on a single source.
- Shared Expenses: By sharing household expenses, the family can significantly reduce individual financial burdens.
- Increased Savings: Combined incomes and shared expenses lead to higher savings, which can be invested for greater returns.

- Diverse Investments: With more financial resources, the family can diversify investments, reducing risk and enhancing growth potential.
- Passive Income: Passive investments generate income without requiring active management, providing financial stability and growth.

Steps to Implement Family-Driven Investing

1. Assess the Existing Portfolio:
   - Review Investments: Analyse the current family portfolio to understand its composition, performance, and areas for improvement.
   - Identify Goals: Set clear financial goals for the family, such as retirement, education, or buying a home.

2. Create a Family Investment Plan:
   - Investment Strategy: Develop an investment strategy that aligns with the family's financial goals and risk tolerance.
   - Asset Allocation: Diversify the portfolio across different asset classes to mitigate risk and maximize returns.
   - Regular Contributions: Establish a system for regular contributions from each family member to grow the investment pool.

3. Leverage Individual Jobs:
   - Stable Employment: Encourage each family member to pursue stable employment or careers that provide a steady income.
   - Skill Development: Invest in education and skill development to enhance earning potential and career growth.
   - Job Benefits: Take advantage of job benefits, such as retirement plans, health insurance, and employee stock options.

4. Share Household Expenses:

- Budgeting: Create a family budget that outlines shared expenses and individual contributions.
- Cost-Saving Measures: Implement cost-saving measures, such as bulk purchasing, energy efficiency, and reducing unnecessary expenses.
- Emergency Fund: Build a family emergency fund to cover unexpected expenses and financial emergencies.

5. Invest Collectively:

- Passive Investments: Focus on passive investment options, such as index funds, mutual funds, and real estate, which require minimal active management.
- Regular Reviews: Conduct regular reviews of the investment portfolio to monitor performance and make necessary adjustments.
- Long-Term Focus: Maintain a long-term investment perspective, avoiding short-term market fluctuations and focusing on sustained growth.

Examples of Successful Family-Driven Investing

To illustrate the potential of family-driven investing, consider the following examples:

1. Real Estate Investments:

- Rental Properties: The family pools funds to purchase rental properties, generating passive rental income and benefiting from property appreciation.
- Real Estate Investment Trusts (REITs): Investing in REITs allows the family to gain exposure to real estate markets without the need for active property management.

2. Stock Market Investments:

- Index Funds: Investing in index funds provides diversified exposure to the stock market, reducing risk and ensuring steady growth.

- Dividend Stocks: Focusing on dividend-paying stocks generates regular income, which can be reinvested to grow the portfolio further.

3. Small Business Investments:
   - Franchises: The family invests in franchise opportunities, benefiting from a proven business model and brand recognition.
   - Local Businesses: Supporting and investing in local businesses with high growth potential can yield significant returns.

Overcoming Potential Challenges

Family-driven investing is not without its challenges. Here are some common issues and how to address them:
1. Differing Opinions:
   - Open Communication: Foster open communication and regular family meetings to discuss investment decisions and address concerns.
   - Decision-Making Framework: Establish a clear decision-making framework, such as voting or consensus, to ensure fair and objective choices.

2. Financial Discrepancies:
   - Transparent Contributions: Ensure transparency in financial contributions and expenses, with clear records and accountability.
   - Equal Opportunity: Provide equal opportunities for all family members to contribute and benefit from the investments.

3. Generational Differences:
   - Education and Training: Educate younger family members about financial management and investing to ensure continuity and informed decision-making.
   - Involvement: Involve all generations in the investment process, encouraging input and participation from everyone.

Guide to Millions

Starting your investment journey with your family offers a unique opportunity to build on an existing portfolio, leverage individual incomes, and share expenses for greater financial growth. By adopting a strategy where each family member has their own job while contributing to shared investments, you can create a stable, diversified, and growth-oriented financial foundation.

The key to success lies in open communication, clear goals, and a collective commitment to the family's financial well-being. By working together, you can achieve financial milestones more quickly, secure a prosperous future for future generations, and continue the legacy of family-driven wealth building.

Chapter 4.3
FAMILY OFFICES AND LEGACY BUILDING:
Protecting and Growing Wealth for Future Generations

Building wealth as a family is not just about accumulating assets; it's about creating a lasting legacy that supports and enriches future generations. One of the most effective ways to achieve this is through the establishment of a family office. Family offices play a crucial role in protecting investments and assets, ensuring that each family member is taken care of while wealth continues to grow. This chapter delves into the concept of family offices, the use of family trusts, and the importance of professional management in sustaining family wealth.

Understanding Family Offices

A family office is a private organization established to manage the wealth and financial affairs of a wealthy family. It provides a range of services, including investment management, estate planning, tax services, philanthropy, and family governance. Family offices are designed to serve the unique needs of affluent families, ensuring their wealth is preserved, grown, and passed down through generations.

Types of Family Offices:
- Single-Family Office (SFO): Serves one wealthy family, providing personalized services tailored to their specific needs.
- Multi-Family Office (MFO): Serves multiple wealthy families, offering a broader range of services while sharing costs and resources.

Key Functions of a Family Office:
- Investment Management: Overseeing the family's investment portfolio, including asset allocation, risk management, and performance monitoring.

- Estate Planning: Ensuring a smooth transfer of wealth to future generations through trusts, wills, and other legal structures.
- Tax Planning: Implementing tax-efficient strategies to minimize liabilities and maximize wealth retention.
- Philanthropy: Managing charitable activities and ensuring the family's philanthropic goals are met.
- Family Governance: Establishing structures and processes for decision-making, conflict resolution, and maintaining family unity.

Protecting Wealth through Family Trusts

One of the primary tools used by family offices to protect and manage wealth is the family trust. A family trust is a legal entity that holds and manages assets on behalf of the family members. It provides numerous benefits, including asset protection, tax efficiency, and control over wealth distribution.

Benefits of Family Trusts:
- Asset Protection: Shields family assets from creditors, legal claims, and financial risks, ensuring long-term security.
- Tax Efficiency: Offers tax advantages by distributing income in a tax-efficient manner and utilizing various tax planning strategies.
- Wealth Distribution: Controls how and when assets are distributed to beneficiaries, ensuring that wealth is used responsibly and according to the family's wishes.
- Privacy: Maintains confidentiality regarding the family's financial affairs, as trusts are not subject to public disclosure.

Types of Family Trusts:
- Revocable Trust: Can be altered or revoked by the grantor during their lifetime, providing flexibility in managing assets.

- Irrevocable Trust: Cannot be changed once established, offering stronger asset protection and tax benefits.
- Discretionary Trust: Gives trustees the discretion to decide how and when beneficiaries receive distributions, based on predefined criteria.
- Generation-Skipping Trust: Designed to pass wealth directly to grandchildren, bypassing the children's generation to reduce estate taxes.

Professional Management in Family Offices

As family wealth grows, managing it becomes increasingly complex. Professional management within a family office ensures that the family's financial affairs are handled with expertise and diligence. This can include hiring financial advisors, investment managers, tax professionals, and legal experts to provide specialized services.

Advantages of Professional Management:

- Expertise: Access to skilled professionals with specialized knowledge in investment management, tax planning, legal matters, and more.
- Objectivity: Professional managers provide unbiased advice and decision-making, reducing the influence of family dynamics on financial matters.
- Efficiency: Streamlined processes and systems for managing investments, expenses, and reporting, enhancing overall efficiency.
- Risk Management: Comprehensive risk management strategies to protect the family's assets and ensure long-term financial stability.
- Continuity: Ensures that wealth management continues seamlessly across generations, preserving the family's legacy.

Building a Legacy with Family Offices

Creating a lasting family legacy requires more than just financial management; it involves instilling values, fostering unity, and ensuring that future generations are well-prepared to manage and grow the family's wealth. Family offices play a pivotal role in this process by providing education, governance structures, and support for family members.

Key Components of Legacy Building:
- Family Education: Educating family members about financial literacy, investment principles, and the responsibilities of wealth management. This includes regular family meetings, workshops, and access to financial advisors.
- Family Governance: Establishing a family constitution or charter that outlines the family's values, mission, and governance structures. This document serves as a guide for decision-making, conflict resolution, and maintaining family unity.
- Philanthropy and Social Responsibility: Encouraging and supporting philanthropic activities that align with the family's values. This not only gives back to the community but also instils a sense of social responsibility in future generations.
- Succession Planning: Preparing the next generation to take on leadership roles within the family office and ensuring a smooth transition of responsibilities.

Case Studies of Successful Family Offices:
1. The Rockefeller Family Office: One of the most well-known family offices, the Rockefeller family office has successfully managed and grown the family's wealth for over a century. It focuses on diversified investments, philanthropy, and preserving the family's legacy.
2. The Walton Family Office: The Walton family, founders of Walmart, have established a family office that manages their vast wealth through investments in various sectors, including retail, technology, and real estate. The office also supports philanthropic initiatives and family governance.

3. The Pritzker Family Office: The Pritzker family, known for their ownership of the Hyatt hotel chain, has a family office that manages investments in private equity, real estate, and other assets. The office also emphasizes education and leadership development for family members.

Establishing a family office and leveraging family trusts are powerful strategies for protecting and growing family wealth across generations. By providing comprehensive financial management, expert advice, and a focus on legacy building, family offices ensure that each family member is taken care of while the family's wealth continues to rise.

The key to success lies in combining professional management with a strong emphasis on family values, education, and governance. By doing so, families can create a lasting legacy that not only preserves wealth but also empowers future generations to continue building on the foundation laid by their predecessors.

In summary, starting your investment journey with a family office provides a structured and strategic approach to managing wealth. It offers the benefits of professional expertise, asset protection, and tax efficiency, while fostering family unity and ensuring the responsible use of wealth. With careful planning and a focus on legacy, family offices can help families achieve financial security and prosperity for generations to come.

HELP WITH INVESTING

How We Can Help

Embarking on the journey to becoming a millionaire by saving and investing in property and private businesses is a formidable yet achievable goal. However, balancing this ambition with work, family obligations, or a lack of expertise can be challenging. This is where Horvat Capital steps in to assist you.

Our Vision

At Horvat Capital, we envision democratizing wealth creation by empowering individuals and businesses to thrive through tailored financial solutions. We believe in a future where every person and business can unlock their full financial potential. Our mission is to be the leading provider of holistic wealth management solutions, offering the expertise and resources you need to navigate today's dynamic financial landscape.

Tailored Financial Solutions

Horvat Capital's approach is designed to help you strategically build a diversified portfolio of properties and private businesses. Our experienced team works diligently to identify high-potential investment opportunities that align with your financial goals. Whether you are a novice investor or someone with experience, our tailored strategies will guide you towards achieving substantial returns with minimal risk.

Empowering Your Financial Growth

Our vision drives us to continuously innovate and adapt, ensuring we remain at the forefront of industry trends and developments. By empowering you to build robust portfolios, we aim to create a more inclusive and equitable financial ecosystem. We believe wealth creation should be accessible to all, enabling small businesses to thrive and individuals to achieve their financial aspirations.

How We Operate

1. Investment Strategy: We prioritize investments in essential services such as healthcare, utilities, and food production, ensuring consistent demand even during economic downturns.

2. Expert Management: Our team of seasoned professionals manages every aspect of your investments, from acquisition to growth optimization, ensuring you receive consistent returns.

3. Transparency and Communication: Regular updates and detailed reports keep you informed about the performance of your investments, providing peace of mind and confidence in your financial journey.

4. Flexible Investment Options: With investment periods ranging from 1 to 5 years and a minimum investment threshold, we offer flexibility to suit your financial needs and goals.

Achieve Your Financial Goals

At Horvat Capital, we are committed to turning our vision into reality, one client at a time. By partnering with us, you can leverage our expertise to build wealth strategically and efficiently. Our holistic wealth management solutions are designed to help you navigate the complexities of investing in property and private businesses, ensuring you are well on your way to becoming a millionaire within 10 years.

Join Us Today

If you are interested in reaching your financial aspirations, we are here to help. Visit us at www.horvatcapital.com.au to learn more about how Horvat Capital can support you in achieving your financial goals. Together, we can create a future where wealth creation is within everyone's reach.

Embarking on the path to financial independence and wealth creation is a rewarding journey. With Horvat Capital by your side, you can confidently pursue your goal of becoming a millionaire. Let us handle the complexities of investing, so you can focus on enjoying the rewards of your financial success

www.ingramcontent.com/pod-product-compliance
Lightning Source LLC
Chambersburg PA
CBHW072151070526
44585CB00015B/1093